Dedication

To my wonderful friend,

Joyce Heck.

Thank you for all of your support in my writing and publishing efforts.

You are the best!.
May God be with you and help you always and in all ways!

Why Democrats Hate God?

There is little doubt that God is not a Democrat favorite.

There are many reasons why Democrats hate God including the obvious that some Democrats are atheists. Another big reason in the last two years according to a number of popular preachers has something to do with God selecting Donald Trump to Save America and Americans. By now, those of us who like what Trump is doing for America know that Mr. Trump was sent from God as the people's answer to deep anti-establishment anger and discontent and also as a beacon for goodness. Since Democrats hate Trump, having God as the reason for Trump is reason enough for Democrats to hate God.

"Millions of Americans." declared Dallas megachurch pastor Robert Jeffries in 2017, "believe the election of President Trump represented God giving us another chance—perhaps our last chance—to truly make America great again. Our job was to elect him once God showed us the way." We thank Our Lord to this day that we did. You can bet than any Democrat listening to Jeffries was seething.

Christian Leaders prophesied before the election that God had raised up Donald Trump to lead the nation through a time of crisis.

This gave Democrats another reason to hate God because as the world knows, they already hated Trump. Donald Trump got elected because someone such as God or a legion of Guardian Angels whispered in the individual ears of millions of Americans. The voice(s) said that together in the 2016 election, the people would make a difference, and then God gave Donald Trump to America to be that difference.

The people trusted this self-made Billionaire to do what was best for America and not the bidding of slimy politicians or political donors and hacks. This drove Democrats and allies in the Swamp nuts and it caused intense hate for Trump among them.

The Democrats and the establishment also began to stoke up their hate for the people who supported Trump—the ne'er-do-wells from the basket of deplorables. All were connected to God and so the hate for God became widespread among the Democrats.

For the people looking for an end to progressive rule, Donald Trump was the only candidate for president who offered Americans a breath of fresh air. The people had had enough of the stodgy, bossy, establishment elites in both the Democratic and Republican Parties.

Trump defied the status quo of rich donors controlling the government for their personal benefit. Donald Trump became a great gift from God himself. As the hate for Trump began to boil, the Democrat's hate for God increased in parallel.

You are going to love this book. It explains why Democrats hate God so much.

BRIAN W. KELLY

Title **Why Democrats Hate God?**

Subtitle: *There is little doubt that God is __not__ a Democrat favorite.*

Copyright © November 2018   Brian W. Kelly

Editor: Brian P. Kelly

Author: Brian W. Kelly

Published by:	LETS GO PUBLISH!
Editor	Brian P. Kelly
Editor	Brian P. Kelly
Cover Design	Brian W Kelly
Web site	www.letsgopublish.com

Library of Congress Copyright Information Pending
Book Cover Design by Brian W. Kelly

ISBN Information: The International Standard Book Number (ISBN) is a unique machine-readable identification number, which marks any book unmistakably. The ISBN is the clear standard in the book industry. 159 countries and territories are officially ISBN members. Official ISBN for this book is also on the outside cover:

978-1-947402-67-6

The price for this work is: **$9.95 USD**

10   9   8   7   6   5   4   3   2   1

Release Date: November 2018

Acknowledgments

In every book that I write or edit, I publicly acknowledged all of the help that I have received from many sources. Some of these wonderful people are still on earth and others have made their way to heaven.

I would like to thank many people for helping me in this effort. I appreciate all the help that I received in putting this book together, along with the 183 other books from the past.

My printed acknowledgments were once so large that book readers needed to navigate too many pages to get to page one of the text. To permit me more flexibility, I put my acknowledgment list online at www.letsgopublish.com. The list of acknowledgments continues to grow. Believe it or not, it once cost about a dollar more to print each book.

Thank you all on the big list in the sky and God bless you all for your help.

Please check out www.letsgopublish.com to read the latest version of my heartfelt acknowledgments updated for this book. Thank you all!

In this book, I received some extra special help from many avid Lets Go Publish! supporters including Joyce Heck, Dennis Grimes, Gerry Rodski, Angel Brent Evans, Angel Jim Faller, Wily Ky Eyely, Angel Irene McKeown Kelly, Angel Edward Joseph Kelly Sr., Angel Edward Joseph Kelly Jr., Ann Flannery, Angel James Flannery Sr., Mary Daniels, Bill Daniels, Angel Robert Garry Daniels, Angel Sarah Janice Daniels, Angel Punkie Daniels, Joe Kelly, Diane Kelly, Brian P. Kelly, Mike P. Kelly, Seamus McDuff, Katie P. Kelly, Angel Ben Kelly, and Budmund (Buddy) Arthur Kelly.

Preface

Here we are citizens in a truly exceptional country. Yet, even here in America all is not perfect. As bad as it may be, most Americans never expected the Democrats to begin to take it out on God.

The Democrats definitely have come to hate God. There is no doubt about that.

Where did all this hate come from? It seems like it is just in the past few years that the odor of hate in America is strong enough (if you'll pardon me) to knock a buzzard off a "sh--" wagon. To use a big word to describe it. It is palpable. The Democrats hate God. Everybody knows it but when asked, they have so little regard for the truth. Democrats will deny it.

Can we do anything about it? Well, one thing is for sure, if *"we the people"* as a group do not smarten up, things will get a lot worse and they may never get better again. In this book, we recognize that Democrats are the biggest haters of all things in in America. If we could convince them to find another country to destroy, that would be a fine start.

We do tell them in this book beginning right now to STOP THE HATE! It solves nothing! Dear Democrats. You can't do it alone. While Trump is making America great again, it is time for you and your Party to begin to love God again. Try talking to the Lord Jesus Christ every day for starters if you want your luck to turn.

America has its share of issues for sure, but we are still free to change the country through the election process and of course, we can also start by changing ourselves. Democrats need a changing! According to the founders, it was not supposed to be this way. There is a lot of reason to feel hate today – mostly because there is a lot of hate being thrown at everybody by a lot of Democrats and their sycophant media.

We see no love for regular Americans coming from the mostly miserable, always unhappy media outlets such as The ugly Grey Lady New York Times; MSNBC; and CNN. I used to blame the mainstream media but let's face it, MSNBC, CNN, and the New York Times are responsible for most of the lies and the hate in America today. Let's call it as we see it. They hear the Democrat lies and like as if they are true, they publish. This media is controlled by evil and they have no conscience.

The most recent best thing that has happened to America is that after watching for years Democrats dismantle the good in America, even during Republican Administrations, God intervened and gave us all another chance. He sent his beloved Son over two thousand years ago and though that helped, just recently, God saw that things do not stay right in mankind for too many years at a time.

This time, he found a playboy rogue out in the fields of fun and prosperity in America and he let this rogue know that he had a big job for him. Donald Trump, who did not need God's job offer as life was treating him good already, chose to accept the offer and he ran for President of the US and now he is here with us and we better not blow this opportunity to do the right thing for God. Stop the hate!

Ironically, the person sent to America to help stop the hate and turn our country into something that as in the days of the founders could be great again, has seemingly caused more hate from poor-loser Democrats than any mere mortal would have ever imagined.

God had to know the hate was coming but he hoped we would all figure out how to contain it and assure that the gift from God himself, Donald J. Trump Jr. would be used to gobble up the hate and help set America on a course to be great again--in both material ways and spiritual ways. Instead, in addition to hating Trump, the newly caustic, nasty, dirty Democrat Party began to tell working class workers, Trump and even God, that they simply did not matter.

Power is the only thing that matters to the Democrat hate machine. God gave the power to Trump so Democrats believe they are obligated to hate God the Father, Son, and Holy Ghost. Oh, yes, there are other reasons why Democrats hate God. We will present them and debunk them in this book written by an American for Americans. Democrats would do themselves well to read this book, since there is only one God and even Democrats have just one soul.

And, yes, Virginia, there is just one Hell also, but it is large enough to fit all the hate mongering Democrats if they choose to continue to waddle in the swill. God would love it, however, if at the end of time, there was a lot of open space in Hades. Stop the hate!

You are going to love this book since it is designed by an American for Americans. Few books are a must-read but Why Democrats Hate God will quickly appear at the top of America's most read list. If we do not gain back the greatness of our America, with the right amount of love v hate, with the help of willing, ahem, God-loving Democrats, somebody may come along one day and have no problem taking this great country from us?

Sincerely,

Brian P. Kelly, Editor

Table of Contents

About the Author

Brian W. Kelly retired as an Assistant Professor in the Business Information Technology (BIT) program at Marywood University, where he also served as the IBM i and midrange systems technical advisor to the IT faculty. Kelly has designed, developed, and taught many college and professional courses. He is also a contributing technical editor to a number of IT industry magazines, including "The Four Hundred" and "Four Hundred Guru" published by IT Jungle.

Kelly is a former IBM Senior Systems Engineer and he has been a candidate for US Congress and the US Senate from Pennsylvania. He has an active information technology consultancy. He is the author of 176 books and hundreds of articles. Kelly is a frequent speaker at COMMON, IBM conferences, and other technical conferences. Ask him to speak at your next conservative / nationalist rally!

Over the past thirty years, Brian Kelly has become America's most outspoken and most eloquent conservative protagonist. Besides *Boost Social Security Now!; Taxation Without Representation; and Millennials Are People Too!,* Kelly is also the author of _No Amnesty! No Way!,_ and many other patriotic books.

Endorsed by the Independence Hall Tea Party in 2010, Kelly ran for Congress against a 13-term Democrat; he took no campaign contributions, spent enough to buy signs and T-shirts, and as a virtual unknown, he captured 17% of the vote— www.briankellyforcongress.com.

In 2012, and again briefly in 2018, Kelly launched a write-in campaign www.briankellyforussenate.com. Kelly then reevaluated and wholeheartedly supports Republican challenger Lou Barletta, a conservative leader on immigration policy. Kelly had helped Lou win a resounding victory in the 2010 general election. Kelly is again backing Barletta and John Chrin. Lou Barletta is now running for the US Senate in PA. Like you, Barletta and Chrin love America and think the country with Donald Trump at the helm is great!.

Chapter 1 It Is Not Good to Hate God.

Haters will broadcast your failures, but whisper your success.

LoveOfLifeQuotes.com

Everybody who is anybody admits that there are very few Republican atheists or perhaps better said, atheist Republicans. If you find an atheist Republican, there is speculation that you will have discovered a combination that seems so rare, it could be covered by the Endangered Species Act. So, in terms of Republicans hating God, it is not worth the effort to study. Look on the other side of the aisle.

As far as Democrats hating God, there are many reasons why this has happened. For example, Democrats are significantly more likely to be atheists than Republicans or the rest of the American population. We do know that they not only exist, atheist Democrats exist in some level of abundance.

Moreover, for some unexplained reason, many atheists express a strong hatred of God. Thus there is a likelihood that an atheist Democrat would by definition, hate God.

Nonetheless, to some this is very clear, but to those who study matters such as this, they are at a loss to explain the phenomenon of an atheist hating God. Yet, they do and all you have to do is check the atheist blogs such as commonsenseatheism.com.

Here is the conundrum. How can you hate someone you don't believe in? Is that not a puzzlement? Why should you feel any hostility? If God really does not exist, would it not be expected that atheists would just relax and seek a good time before they become digested by the soil at life's end?

In other words, to an atheist, why should it matter if people believe in God? Carrying this to a logical conclusion would be that if atheism is true, then nothing matters.

Aldous Huxley (1894-1963) was a major English writer, novelist, and philosopher. He is the brother of the atheistic evolutionist Sir Julian Huxley, and the author of the highly read novel *A Brave New World*. He advocated a drug-fueled utopia and had some similarities of thinking to his brother Julian. In his writings, Aldous offers some reasons for his anti-Christian stance:

"I had motive for not wanting the world to have a meaning ... the philosophy of meaninglessness was essentially an instrument of liberation, sexual and political."

Huxley had little interest in moral constraints. Many who hate God want nothing to do with constraints. They would prefer a world in which they can make up their own rules or have no rules at all. If God does not exist, why not have it your way?

Experts have concluded that the secret to their unhappiness as atheists is that they are uncertain of their beliefs. How can we know anything about a subject that is virtually impossible to definitively prove or disprove?

So, in frustration perhaps, they hate God and Christians because they have no concrete level of confidence that God does not exist. Moreover, they are jealous of Christians who find solace in their belief of God. Did I say that?

Seeing Christians must remind them to some extent that they are *suppressing the truth*. Recent work by students of atheism, present arguments that there are far more non-believers in God in the modern era than ever before.

What does it mean if we find that 69 percent of Americans say a belief in God is an important part of being American? What about the other 31%?

Recent surveys have found that only one in ten Americans say that they do not believe in God. Less than that, a paltry 3 percent identify as atheist. However, there is always a new study when data is inconclusive and/or changing. I found a new study that does suggest that the true number of atheists could be much larger that 3%, perhaps even 10 times larger than previously estimated.

The fact that the study of God and the study of no-God (atheism) is ongoing means that the analysts must do their work in a condition of flux. Additionally as more researchers take up the mission, their various methods will differ as will their results.

In this book, we explore the *why* of a well-studied phenomenon. Our reporting is on Democrats and a major premise is that there are so many who hate God that is not outlandish to generically conclude that *Democrats hate God.*

There are a number of sources for example that tell a story about 29% of Americans who identify themselves as Democrat. Similar sources conclude that 66% of atheists identify as Democrat. Working through all the analysis and theories by the numbers, a popularly accepted percentage of atheists in America is 3.1% of the population. But admittedly today this may be off by a factor of 10. Thus these are all theories and their basis is as solid as mush. But let's carry this math a bit further.

Since 2/3 (66%) of the atheists are Democrats, that means that (3.1 x 0.666 =) 2.066% of the population is both Democrat and atheist. And so, if 2.066% of the population are atheist Democrats and 29% of the population are Democrats, that would mean that (2.066 / 29 =) 0.07126 or 7.126% of Democrats are atheist. Of course as in all imperfect research, that conclusion may not be right.

When credible sources such as the Pew Research Center think 9% of the population meets the technical definition of being an atheist, this would make 20.69 percent of self-identifying Democrats--what might be called "definition atheists".

Consequently, there is a very big difference depending on how you calculate who is a Democrat and who is an atheist. For our purposes, let's just say that a significant number of Democrats are atheists and they may hate God simply because they are atheists. So for sure, these Democrats could *legimately* say they hate God because they are atheists.

When atheists are together, even in electronic surroundings such as chat rooms, they like to talk about their atheism. They like it when they all think alike. So, if a non-non-believer such as a practicing Christian begins to engage them in conversation, the outcome is not always pleasant. For example, the visitor might be repeatedly insulted; told that they are stupid, that they can't think properly; mocked; cussed, etc.

Christians believe that atheists have neither fact nor logic on their side. And so one suffering in such a chat room would always get a noteworthy response to the question "Why do you atheists hate God?" Noteworthy is civil as the response would inevitably be foul language, insults, lies, misrepresentations, hatred, condemnation, and worse perhaps. Check it out if you find interest in the topic.

Though atheists hate the idea of God , it follows that they also hate those who believe they are wrong. Consequently, once engaged, they most often end the discussion by saying "We don't hate what does not exist!" That is clever, but they do.

How do you know when you hate someone? In my book, *The Cure for Hate !!!* , I explore the idea of hate quite extensively. The fact is that when you hate someone, you tend to speak evil of them, say negative things about them, call them names, accuse them of bad stuff, etc. Verbal condemnations reveal how a person feels about someone, so once a dialogue begins, the hate typically flows.

The behavior of atheists to non-non-believers is much like their same behavior aimed at God. It demonstrates their hatred for God. Atheists like to condemn the God of Scripture and their numerous hate-filled chats are full of condemnations for the God of the Bible. It is their schtick shall we say.

Not all atheists react in the same way. Therefore, these are simply my personal generalities. However, those with much experience in such analysis would conclude that an atheist's regular condemnation of God, their accusations of his immorality, speaking evil of him, etc., clearly demonstrates that they hate God. And, a super majority of Democrat atheists hate God. I would say with that I have proven my point in the title: "Why Democrats Hate God.".

What about Democrat non-atheists? Do they hate God?

It depends!

The hate for God of Democrat atheists is not necessarily the same type of hate as Democrat non-atheists. Those Democrat non-atheists who hate God certainly have God tucked way back in their minds. They do not profess atheism but they are also not too inclined about hanging out in the church basement for a Sunday Social, so they can mingle with other "believers." In fact, they are not inclined to be church goers at all. They hate God simply because HE is in the way.

In the next chapter, we explore this idea in greater detail. The incident that most clearly shows that many Democrats, far more than you might think—who are not atheists have a big reason to hate God has to do with the fact that those who love God are beating them or at least challenging them in a power game that the Democrats believe they must win. How can that be?

Well, when you explore the percentages of other types of Americans such as practicing Christians and those to whom God has substantial meaning in their lives, they outnumber the Democrats. Even if a one-time poll shows that they may not outnumber Democrats on a given day, they are a substantial number. They are a substantial number of individuals who do not espouse the liberal progressive, socialist, and in fact, the leftist agenda, which Republicans might simply call the Democrat Agenda. These God lovers are anti-Democrat. If my name were Brian, I would not necessarily be inclined to love anti-Brian's.

God lovers are thus not friends of Democrats because they love God. If it were up to them, God lovers would use their God to outlaw the precepts of the Democrat Party. Thus they are enemies of Democrats. Thus, their God is the enemy of Democrats and is a threat to the well-being of the Party. Thus it is perfectly natural that they hate God. When they pass away, they may wish to suggest that they were always God lovers. But, then again, God does not have a strong affinity towards liars.

Chapter 2 If God is Dead; Why Hate Him?

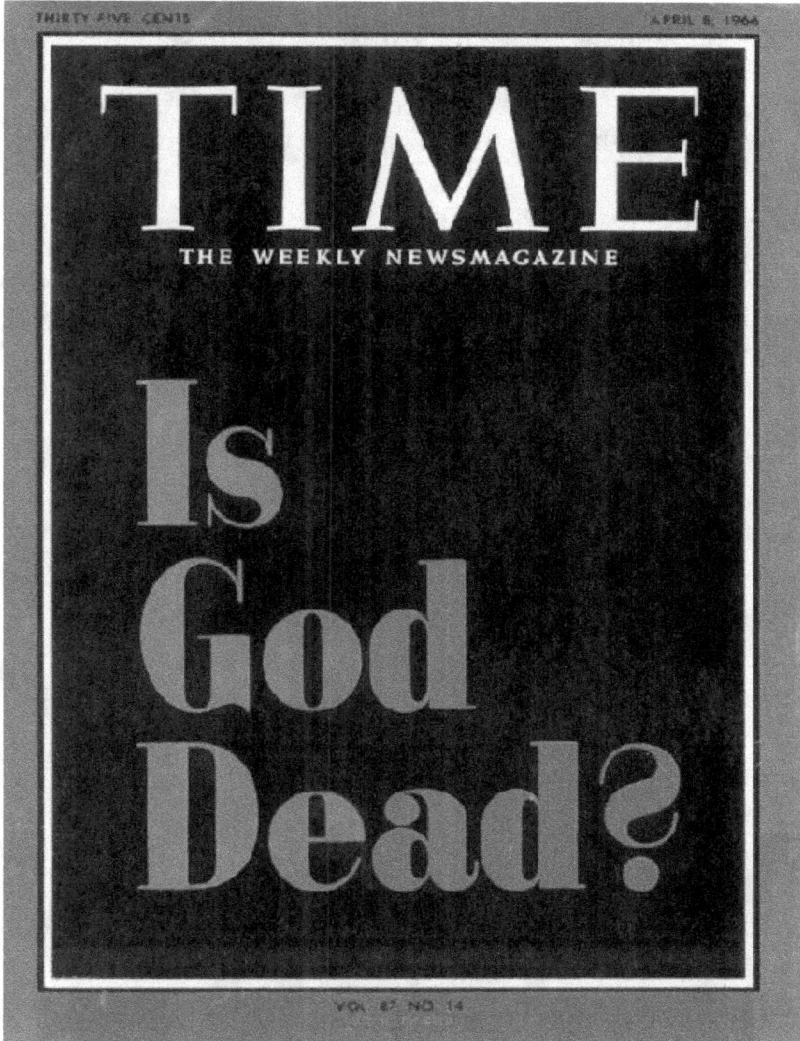

Along with many who are far more religious than I ever hope to be, especially after the Kavanaugh hearings, more Americans from both major parties are asking: "What ever happened to Democratic Party?" Among the many are well known faith leaders such as Rev. Franklin Graham. The Reverend Graham is in a quandry as to what has become of the Democratic Party—especially with its frequently exposed anti-God and anti-America agenda.

If we were not all seeing it with our own eyes, we would not believe it. Yet there it is in full bloom on the streets; in the media and right in our faces. Wake up in the morning and watch the agnostic media—especially with its frequently exposed anti-God and anti-America agenda. What brought us to this? The Party of mobs has lost its way.

The Democrat Party was once the party of the people. Workers once looked to the Democrat Party to protect them all from corporate labor bullies. Today, it is well acknowledged by scholars that over two sets of terms, with a Bush in between, Presidents Bill Clinton and Barack Obama helped shift power away from the people towards corporations. It was this big change in focus that many believe created a big opening for a guy like Donald Trump to enter as an American hero.

Nobody was representing the people. Democrat leadership gave it up. Donald Trump's populist and nationalist inclinations were a healing balm for an America subsumed by an insidious "what's the use" sense of failure.

The president of the Billy Graham Evangelistic Association (BGEA) has taken to social media to air his concern about Democrats forcing a county party leader to resign a while back over posting a statement that most Americans would -- and should – feel proud to make:

"I stand for the flag, I kneel at the cross," former United States Marine and Gulf War veteran Mark Salvas declared – to the chagrin of his fellow Democratic leaders, according to World Net Daily (WND).

There is irony in almost everything. For example, Billy Graham, was a well-known registered member of the Democratic Party when the Party was worthy of that "ic" at the end. In today's Mobs v Jobs Democrat world, I think the elder Graham would have run from the D Party faster than the speed of light.

Ecumenism was not on the agenda of many sects back in those days and so Graham, Sr, in 1960 was 100% opposed to the candidacy of John F. Kennedy. He feared that because Kennedy was a Catholic, he would be bound to follow the Pope. Would it not be nice if that was the biggest problem Democrats had with God today?

Franklin Graham of course is the son of the late iconic evangelist. Like Donald Trump, Graham is quite adept at using social media. He offered commentary that backed the veteran Salvas, hoping to shame Democrats for punishing their own party member from Graham's perspective—for making such an honorable pro-American declaration.

Graham took to Facebook to say: "I'm not ashamed of my patriotism – not one bit." The Reverend has millions of followers. "I fought for this country. I think I have a right to have a voice and be patriotic." Graham reaffirmed his complete support of Salvas and he questioned the motivation taking over the Democrat Party—one that many see as continuing to move farther and farther to the left, further from country and further from God.

Graham continues to ask: "What has happened to the Democrat Party?" Like many others, he has begun to think that the Party has evolved so far left, they can't be made right? Hard as it is to believe, the one-time party of American workers has begun to equate loyalty to God and America, especially whites, to *racism*.

Democrat leaders were not upset just at Salvas' taking a stance on his patriotism but they were noticeably distraught when Salvas publicly proclaimed his personal faith as the new chairman of the Allegheny County Democratic Party. They were so furious that they booted him from his position. Having Salvas, a patriot and a lover of God, as a member, was too much for the Democrats to take.

Now, I would have been asking many times in this book, "Do Democrats hate God?" However, because it appears to me that the answer is self-evident, I will substitute an interrogative statement: "Why Democrats hate God?" What could God have possibly done to them for them all of a sudden to be putting their immortal souls on the line?

Regarding the Salvas issue, initially, there was little information as to why. Once the party of tolerance, the Democratic Party is plain old intolerant today. In addition to being against deep patriotism and personal faith in God, whites and blacks in the Party have developed an unusual form of anti-white bias and hate. Amazing!

When Salvas was interviewed by a Fox News show host, Todd Starnes, he offered his take on how angered Democratic Party leaders were about Salvas' wife showing her support in a Facebook post for a police officer who was accused of killing an African American with supposed racist intent.

When today's Democrats cannot explain why they hate anybody without cause, they resort to calling them a racist. They think we believe them. Hmmph! I would suggest they call them *wolf* instead, as there is no impact anymore for the word *racist* as it is simply Democrats in frustration from not winning, calling "wolf."

Democrats are big on purging even their own for nothing more than an accusation. Guilt or innocence seems to no longer matter, if accused of anything.

Even though the support offered by his wife in this case was clearly expressed to denote her confidence in the law enforcement officer— because she had witnessed his virtuous character all his life, since she was accused of something—anything, she had to be declared *guilty*.

Democrats interpreted her backing the law enforcement officer as nothing more than a white supremacist rant. And so, here we have another major issue for Democrats—law enforcement. Nobody loves a criminal as an entity group but Democrats. There could be no explanation to satisfy the Democratic hate after that. Democrats hate law-enforcement. So, the lady had to pay the price for supporting reason.

"Salvas offered that they [he and his wife] had known the police officer and his family since the officer was a toddler," Fox host Starnes explained to his audience.

Rep. Ed Gainey (D-Pa.) sided with the Democratic leadership and hopped on the Dems race-card bandwagon. Salvas's rationale was unacceptable in the Democrat Kangaroo Court and so he was "legitimately" accused by Gainey of insulting the entirety of African-American voters. For Gainey it was obvious that losing votes—as opposed to genuine concern over racism, was the major issue at hand.

Perhaps if Salvas did not love God and Country and was not white and did not believe in innocence before guilt, and he did not have faith in law-enforcement, he would have had a chance in this Kangaroo Court. However, the Kangaroos are not as smart as real humans.

Gainey offered this reason for his outrage at Salvas: "To put that up on Facebook was, to me, insensitive – also to African Americans, who, as you know, have backed the Democratic Party for quite a long time, and everybody knows that it was insensitive," According to the Todd Starnes Show, Gainey's position was that "A Democratic leader has to be sensitive." The position of all Democrats appears to be if accused, you are guilty so shut up or you will be expunged!

God at the DNC Convention of 2012

The Democrats dislike for God is not new. I remember the 2012 Democratic National Convention that preceded former President Barack Obama's second term. Do you remember that a similar reception was given to the idea of God when a speaker said he knelt at the cross and bowed to the flag. Do you recall his being poorly received? Do we all recall that Democrats in the Convention Center booed after the leadership announced that God was being reintroduced to their party's platform. Such audacity!

You may remember this headline: "Thousands of bloggers are reporting this morning that delegates at the Democratic convention in Charlotte booed when God was reintroduced into their party's platform," CatholicCulture.org reported this in September 2012.

As a one-time avid Democrat, I find little sanity in the Democrat Party of today. I have not changed registrations, but I admit that I now think of myself as a reluctant Democrat. I am however, a very willing follower of Jesus Christ who always trumps petty politics.

The new Democratic Party has chosen to let God behind in its quest to regain national power. I know that I was outraged at what many say was the most memorable moment of the 2012 Democratic National Convention. The delegates denied God three times from the convention floor. In 1992, from the convention floor, the Dems silenced Bob Casey Sr. from PA for loving babies in the womb. They would not let him speak.

Now, in 2018, the son, Casey Jr., who sucked up to Dems and got elected Senator and supports Planned Parenthood's toasting babies for profit, is now trying to say he is pro-life. Sorry Charley! We're smarter than that.

The issue of God's interjection into Democrat Politics back then arose when conservatives slammed Democrats for deleting references to God that had been in the liberals' 2008 platform. To pretend it was a mistake, so the people would not know how Dems really felt about God, the Obama campaign quickly mustered a floor amendment to stuff back-in the clauses in the previously approved 2012 platform.

Those looking on believed it should have been a pro-forma matter, but when convention chairman Antonio Villaraigosa, mayor of Los Angeles, called the vote, the floor responded with a vigorous "no" twice. As muffled as TV reception might present a voice floor vote, it was clear that God had lost. I know what I heard. You know what you heard. The Dems three times had voted God down.

In a fit of procedural integrity, Mr. Villaraigosa tried to get the required two-thirds to amend a third time, but the "no's" were louder than ever.

I heard them. You heard them. You could not miss the "no." I heard Democrats saying no to God and I wondered back then what that was all about. Finally, visibly frustrated, the Chairman, who knew "no" would not stand with Dems who had not yet been convinced God did not matter—lied when he announced that the motion had passed even though everyone in the hall knew by voice, it had not. Politics came before truth.

There is no good reason to reject God.

Why were Democrat delegates generally hostile to God? Back then, there was a perception that God was for Romney and not for Obama. In the latest Gallup numbers at the time, while the convention was continuing, President Obama had a 46 percent advantage over Mitt Romney among those who professed "no religion" but he lagged 23 percent behind Mr. Romney among those who said they are "highly religious."

So, three times they voted no on *God*. Why again? Well, asking a group of Democratic true believers — or in this case, true nonbelievers — whether they wanted God in the platform was for sure their secular equivalent of blasphemy. God had to go. But if anybody knew their real intent, the Democrats would have to go.

The concern was for those Americans who would immediately reject the Democrats if they did not lie about their disdain for God. Obama won because Democrats would not believe their own Party would vote against God. Yet, they did—three times.

Can you imagine if the third "no" vote were truthfully recorded as "no?"

Democrats from coast to coast (including fly-over country) would most likely not have cheered their party devising a godless platform. Elected leaders apparently thought it was a good idea.

"When that original decision was brought to the attention of ordinary American voters – outside the control of the central Democratic Party apparatus, it was unpopular. It did not play well in Peoria," CatholicCulture.org's Phil Lawler explained.

"As we described above, belatedly at best. Reluctantly at worst, the Democratic leaders realized that they should put God back in the picture, so an amendment to the platform was placed on the convention's agenda." You all know how that went down as we described. There were three "no" voice votes before the chairman ignored the last set of voices.

"The leaders wanted God out, but they lied because they did not want to give American voters the opportunity to see just how radical the Democratic Party had become … they wanted the amendment approved quickly."

One might suggest and win bets if challenged that then-Los Angeles Mayor Antonio Villaraigosa was put between a rock and a hard place. He clearly saved the Party. He did well for all who profess the creed of the Democrats. The Chairman not only saved face for his party so that it did not come off as a pack of atheists and anti-Semitists, his actions gave Obama a clean victory over Romney in the General election. Nobody expected lies from Dems but they got them and they swallowed them whole.

"Villaraigosa was clearly lying, in any case – there is no way that the voice vote had passed," Breitbart News explained in September 2012. It was on National TV. Everybody heard the three "no" votes. Afterwards the "no-sayers" were outraged by their own party.

"These opponents stood up and protested, waving and shouting – the fix was in. The Democratic leadership had to ram a mention of God and a mention of Jerusalem through—violating their own rules—to avoid the fallout within their own ranks." Lying has always been very effective for Democrats—as a tool it continues to be used. Believe a Democrat at your own peril.

Franklin Graham continues to be vocal about his support for many of President Donald Trump's conservative Christian policies regarding religious freedom and biblical principles concerning social issues. Graham stands his ground for sure.

Graham made it quite clear earlier this summer in August 2018, that what truly matters is not whether one stands with Republicans or Democrats – but whether one stands with God.

With Democrats standing as far away from God as they possibly can, it will take great people like Franklin Graham to help Americans understand that there is no love lost between the D's and the G's—the Father, Son, and Holy Spirit.

Will the F, S, & Holy G, accept a Democrat apology? It may be moot because nobody expects one to come any time soon. The Democrats are very content hating God. That's how it is.

Chapter 3 God Gave US Donald Trump

God and Trump—hated by Democrats

We have already shown that Democrats hate God and they hate Donald Trump so we won't bother with those topics in this chapter. But it helps to provide more information.

Another reason why Democrats hate God is that many writers and preachers believe that God had something to do with sending Donald Trump to Save America and Americans. God sure did.

And so, it follows that Trump was sent from God as the people's answer to deep anti-establishment anger and discontent and as a beacon for goodness. None of that sits well with hard left Democrats. I do not have to prove that—I know, so I won't waste a page of text right here. You already know it.

"Millions of Americans." declared Dallas megachurch pastor Robert Jeffries in 2017, "believe the election of President Trump represented God giving us another chance—perhaps our last chance—to truly make America great again. Our job was to elect him once God showed us the way."

We thank Our Lord to this day that we did. You can bet than any Democrat linked to the Party's thought machine, listening to Jeffries was seething.

It gave them another reason to hate God because as the world knows, they already hated Trump at the highest level right next to Satanic hate.

Donald Trump got elected because someone, such as God, whispered in the individual ears of millions of American voters. The voice said that together in the 2016 election, the people would make a difference, and then the voice gave Donald Trump to America to be that difference.

The people trusted this self-made Billionaire to do what was best for America and not do the bidding of slimy politicians or political donors and hacks. This drove Democrats and allies in the Swamp nuts and it caused intense hate for Trump among them. Because God gave us Trump, Democrats hate for God intensified.

The Democrats and the establishment also began to stoke up their hate for the people who supported Trump. You know who they are as Obama and Hillary had previously identified them as—the ne'er-do-wells from the basket of deplorables who cling to their guns and bibles. All were connected to God and so the hate for God by Democrat leaders increased and became widespread among all Democrats.

For the people looking for an end to progressive rule, Donald Trump was the only candidate for president who offered Americans a breath of fresh air. The people had had enough of the stodgy, bossy, establishment elites in both the Democratic and Republican Parties. The people knew the Democrat Party offered nothing for them in 2016.

Trump defied the status quo of rich donors controlling the government for their personal benefit. Donald Trump to many, including myself became a great gift from God himself. As the hate for Trump began to boil, the hate for God increased in parallel. Democrat leaders knew that God endorsed Donald Trump but they refused to talk about it with regular Democrats.

All Democrats know that Donald J. Trump loves America and American traditional values. Because the leadership forbids the members from fining any value in the Trump message, patriotism has become a negative attribute for Democrats. If Trump benefits from it, it must be hated, and it must be put down.

Wouldn't we all like to have raised all good kids. Just look at the goodness that Trump instilled into his own children. That is even more reason to hate Trump and his fine children. Democrats do not like anything Trump or anything named Trump. Since God created the Trump children, they too needed to be hated by Democrats and so also the First Lady. Democrats have more than enough hate for God and anything God-like to go around.

Hard as it may be to believe, the Democrats and their allies in the mainstream media have grown to hate the whole Trump family. Yes, as noted they hate even the smallest of Trumps as well as the First Lady. The Democrats operate 24 X 7 to hate God; to hate Trump; to hate the deplorables—especially the white ones; and to hate the Trump family as well as anybody who likes Trump. Choice for Democrats, other than for abortion, is not an option.

Donald Trump sizzles their low-capacity brains and so he causes their hate to intensify because he is undaunted and unfazed by their useless attacks . The fact that God continually gives Trump the strength and competence to attack back and win, simply drives them nuts and boosts their capacity to hate.

Democrats try to get the President to stop tweeting because he uses tweets to defeat them. They try to get him to stop the rallies so their media can control the news. God has made Trump smarter than all Democrats. This God-given President refuses to change and calls the Democrats all out as fakers and their sycophant medias as "fake news."

Trump is not a liberal fool or a progressive socialist tool who hates America. He is simply for America and Americans First. So are you and I, especially if we think about it for a while. Our love for our families, our country, our president and our God infuriates the Democrats whose hate knows no bounds.

Roger Anghis recently said. **Democrats Have Been Given Over To A Reprobate Mind**. I know I have seen it and more than likely you have also. Don't you wish it was not so obvious who they have become?

Democrats have become reprobates regarding their hate for God and all things Trump. Looking for other words to describe their behavior, the list is long and includes many words that are non-complimentary but nonetheless describe the Democrats of 2018 quite well. You know the words corrupt, degenerate, foul, wanton, immoral, improper, incorrigible, lewd, rude, sinful, unprincipled, vile, and of course, wicked. They know who they are, but they hate God regardless.

There is always an election coming every two years for the House and the Senate and every four years for the presidency. It is important that conservatives and evangelicals and all good people and those who love God and who love America—and of course those who have come to accept God's servant Donald Trump as our own, to get out and vote? Don't leave it up to Joe. The insanity that will ensue if Democrats gain power will make the Obama administration look like angelic heaven.

Are the Democrats and the corrupt media one and the same?

Is there any separation between the press and the Democrat Party? Not much if any!!

Students of Revolutionary War history know that Our forefathers intended for there to be a free press. Along with the Executive, Legislative, and Judicial Branches, the press was to be a fourth branch of government. It has thus been termed the fourth estate. Unlike the corrupt press of today, in the 1700's the fourth estate was not tethered to a political party, especially one like the hating, angry-mob known as the Democrat Party

The current version of the fourth estate is not free. It is corrupt and in fact, it is anti-American, and also anti-God. It might as well be the Democrat Party.

The mainstream press still does not like Trump because he represents normal God-loving and God-fearing Americans and not the fringe elements of the country. The press hates Trump and so they hate God. Trump calls out the corrupt press as the fakes that they are. They hate him because he is not controlled by anyone—neither the Democrat Party nor the wimpy swamp-dwelling establishment Republicans.

Neither of these parties give Trump an inch and the Never-Trumper Republicans and the Democrats continue to undermine America by undermining our president. Donald Trump pays close attention to the will of God and Americans are glad that he does. And, so, as noted, this gives Democrats a major cause to hate Trump, God, our country, and all Americans who do not worship at the altar of the Democrats.

You know how bad it is as do the Democrats, but the Democrats have lost their way and the only thing they care about is more power for their Party. They look for anything to disrupt the President even when he is helping their lives while helping the country.

The press never gives him a break and they are always looking for a natural happening to blame on Trump so that they can point him out as a villain. If Mr. Trump, for example, happened to be crossing the street and he stepped off a curb and crushed a newly fallen fully formed beautiful blue robin egg, the press would hang him for being anti-bird, anti-animal, and uncaring. Americans have had enough of such Democrats and are tuned into their chicanery and nastiness.

Meanwhile as we well know, a point which the press will not discuss, when he ran for president, Trump's opponent had gotten four Americans with mothers and fathers back home, killed in Benghazi. At that time and to this day, the biased and corrupt media working with the Democrat Party would not even acknowledge the story.

Something was wrong for more than eight years, and you know what it was. Americans wanted no more of it. We needed Donald Trump and Mike Pence to bring America back to reality and truth. That's "Why

Trump Got Elected!" That's why God intervened in this great 2016 election. That's why the Democrats hate God.

The country's issues included many factors in Obama times--oppressive taxation; legal and illegal immigrants stealing the best jobs; regulations choking businesses; huge debt and deficits shackling our capital resources; a government-run Obamacare system that added taxes and made health worse for Americans as well as corporate offshoring of resources, jobs, and capital.

All of this helped to create a weaker nation. Mrs. Clinton was ready to continue these failed policies. God and the people of our country knew that she supported the same Barack H. Obama's policies, which had created the whole mess in the first place. Only a fool would have given her a chance to run the country.

Additionally, we had a massive energy dependency on our enemies and a Democrat Party that would not permit drilling in the US. We were redistributing wealth from producers to non-producers. We were permitting a huge, growing, inefficient government to operate. It continually lied to the people. It taxed too much and spent way more than it brought in.

Without buying T-shirts, our government had become public enemy # 1 of the people. A good plan, endorsed by Mr. Trump, along with great help from God is now in place and the plan is already saving US from Obama and Clinton perdition. That's "Why God Gave US Trump!" And, that's why the Democrats hate God. When the country succeeds, Democrats get angry. Sad, but true!

God, the answer for us all, rejected by Democrats.

There are many of us who, after crying out for relief for our country for eight years, were convinced in our hearts that God's answer to our pleas for help is Donald Trump. It is up to US now to make sure we make the most of God's great gift. We know for sure that Americans can expect no help from power-hungry, hateful, self-serving Democrats.

As a Democrat, I knew that I was voting for Donald Trump as soon as he broke through the pack of Republicans and began his showdowns with his real opponent, Hillary Clinton. My sister-in-law changed Registrations from Democrat, so that she could vote for Trump in the Primary. There were many like her that loved the country much more than the hateful, angry mob of Democrats who had been running the country.

Like many Democrats, I had had enough of Obama and the Clintons, but my predilection to Trump was more because of him and not because of Clinton negatives. It had more to do with the fact that he reminded me of a last man standing preventing a once-great country from going off a big cliff.

At the end of the day, when the dust had settled, and the battle was over, the last man standing won. Donald Trump won the election despite all odds. Democrats had already crowned Hillary but she never got to sit on the throne. They could not stand Trump's victory and many are still sick over it. In many ways Trump got elected because he was the last man standing between an Obama-like American hell-hole and a return to the Promised Land of our founders.

We thank Our Lord to this day that we all found this President.

Trump represents a welcome change from establishment elitist politics. His great ideas for solving the issues facing America today line up with the thinking of most Americans who are paying attention and who are still affected negatively by the prior administration.

I am glad that you are reading this book, so you too can understand why Donald Trump was not just a default choice for President. I wrote an essay early in the campaign titled, God gave us Donald Trump. I stood by that right through the election and to this day, I feel the same.

Democrats never accepted that they lost. The people voted them out. They continue to try to add Russian characters into their daily soap opera trying to replay and undo the 2016 election.

I took this essay that was published in my local paper and wrote a book out of it that I titled: *God Gave us Donald Trump!* It is available at your favorite online outlets. Democrats have still not forgiven God for sending US Donald J. Trump. They hate God.

Dirty Democrat shenanigans are getting old. Americans are wise to them. I have never been more pleased with a vote than my vote for Donald J. Trump. Thank you, Dear Lord.

Though Democrats train their base to hate our God, our president, and our country, the President is helping all Americans, nonetheless. He has improved life for Blacks, Hispanics, and everybody who depends on a strong economy. He is a great God-fearing man, who continues every day to be an even better president for you, me, and all those who love America.

Democrats think we made a mistake that we will correct when we voted Trump into office. This is not true. We knew what we were doing in 2016 and America is about to do the same again in 2018. Well, those who are not stupid, anyway, and those who do not take orders from the Democrat Party..

Democrats owned the black and Hispanic vote for years simply by promising to help them improve their lives for as long as I can remember. They failed. President Trump has done it in his first two years as well as the rest of all Americans. If unscrupulous Democrats get control of Congress again, all of that stops.

Despite Obama predicting Manufacturing in the US was dead, Trump proved him wrong. Manufacturing jobs, GDP and general economic outlook is rising faster than anyone could have imagined, as well as new and better trade deals and many other factors.

The ress is making up stories about a blue (Democrat) wave hoping to sway the mindless many to vote for the Party that hates America. Why on earth would anyone want to put the brakes on the President simply because he is not politically correct is beyond my grasp and yours too when you think about it.

That is one of the reasons why this President wass elected in the first place and he has done well. It was not an accident. People planned to have Trump as president and we are glad we did. Nobody likes all the things that anybody says, but the results speak for themselves, and more than that, he is right most of the time. I can't understand why anyone would want to "go back" to the days when the dignity of having a job is a bad thing?

The Democrats have embarrassed themselves with their violent rhetoric and actions this round and I shudder to think what would happen if they get any power back. Sen. Tester and Kathleen Williams speak volumes in their silence on this disturbing new trend coming out of their party. Maxine Waters adds to the discord. Democrats love hate too much.

To repeat, Donald Trump knows business and we are already experiencing an enlivened economy in all communities. With substantial foreign business experience, Trump is setting America up as the top dog in the world, and as expected, he is making no apologies.

Trump is a tough American, and he has God on his side. So, we can count on not being pushed around in foreign affairs or delicate negotiations. Our new president as expected, is a winner all the way around. He loves helping all Americans win.

He hates to lose and seldom does. Other than Democrats who continue to play dirty and mean, most of America is very happy that we now have someone in charge who believes in us. Trump believes that we can win and that we will win.

The weaknesses of the Republican Party came out in spades in the primary season and continued as weak-kneed RINOs such as Jeb Bush, John Kasich, and others decided to become tools for the Democrats. During the campaign Donald Trump did not even give them lip service.

In his own way, Mr. Trump told them and all the establishment elites where to go. I like that. I suspect God will get them there eventually. These RINOs and their Progressive Marxist friends across the aisle had been destroying America for their own benefit. It took a guy with guts and stamina to beat them. The last man standing stood against them and won a great victory for the American people. He and God have been wining for us every day since he was elected.

Donald Trump first whooped everybody who was anybody in the GOP. He then ran against a person that some call a withered dishonest fascist--Hillary Clinton. There were many Democrats like me who felt that we could not afford a big liar like Clinton in the White House. We were all in for Donald J. Trump.

As I noted previously, people in my own family who were Democrats all their lives, switched to Republican so they too could vote for Trump in the PA Primary to get on God's side.

For those who can ignore the media's fake news and outright lies, there is plenty to admire about President Trump. Watching his children in action at the GOP convention and the chemistry within the Trump family, Americans got the full sense of what a fine man and a fine dad he is.

Though Trump, like many of us, is not perfect, and if given a chance, he would undo some of his past sins, he does believe in redemption and he continues to enjoy his redemption while he is offering America and Americans a much better life and the promise of a great future.

We need Donald Trump and love

America needs Donald Trump—a businessman and a great negotiator to compete in the world. The former president, Obama, unfortunately for the country found business as a necessary unpleasant evil. Barack Obama chose to have nothing to do with sound business principles while being in charge of the US economy. Hillary Clinton was ready to do more of the same—like a third Term of Obama.

Whether he did or not, the former president gave the impression for years that he had true disdain for America and Americans. It was like he would have loved all Americans to give up their freedoms to become government dependents.

Watching the former president in action, I became convinced that he would have liked America to give up its position as #1 in the world to give other countries more of a chance to beat us. Donald Trump is just the opposite. He is for America to a fault. Trump is clearly for America and Americans-First, and he demonstrated that in his nearly 400 huge campaign rallies before he won the presidency in 2016. Trump in 2016 was a Nationalist / Populist running as a Republican because it made business sense to not go third party

Look at the energy he continues to expend for America. Who besides Donald Trump could do that? In just the last two weeks as of Oct 25, 2018, the President has already had ten rallies for Republican conservative candidates in places all across the United States. Now, he is using his love for America to give him the stamina so that at the rate of five rallies in seven days, he is able to support America-loving candidates across the country. This president is a phenomenon.

Before Trump, we were at the point in our history in which a presidential candidate's position of not being actively opposed to the Bill of Rights was a key selling point for their candidacy.

The GOP today is still full of losers and babies who won't even keep their vows made in the pledge to support the Party's own nominee. No wonder the prior president was treated as an emperor. His sad agenda received no interference from the wimpy GOP.

The scaredy-cat RINOS quaked at the sight of Obama. Then too many of them became Never-Trumpers. To me, they are all losers—especially the Bushes and Marco Rubio, Billy Kristol and George Will, the man with the huge malfunctioning brain. Trump doesn't quake at anything. In fact, he makes me proud to be an American

For years, I had hoped that somebody such as Rush Limbaugh or Donald Trump or somebody with influence and power and money would come along to change our two-party system. I put my vision to words in two books, the first, written five years ago titled, Kill the Republican Party, and the second written in the summer of 2017, titled It's Time for the John Doe Party.

The idea is to rid the party of the swamp and start over again with a new name such as The American Party or The John Doe Party, hoping to attract all current Republican regular people—the 89% who today favor Trump. My plan would leave the RINOS, the Never Trumpers, and the Swamp behind and we would highlight our strong allegiance to God.

I think the new party would attract all Democrats who are like me--pro-American to a fault. It is still a dream yet for many like me as we are watching the disappointing Republican Congress very closely We are very unhappy with Swamp rats such as Paul Ryan and Mitch McConnell, who have ignored us for too many years. I must admit that

McConnel did come through in the Supreme Court confirmation but there is lots he did not do for US.

As much as I am disappointed with many Republicans, I find little saving grace in any of the Democrats. America would be better off with no Democrats until they begin to love God and our country again.

For this ole conservative Democrat, the Republicans for years—even when my dad and I voted together before he died, always seemed to be the better choice than the far-left whacko mob-mentality Democrats. Yet, after Reagan, there were too many bad choices and too many weak men. Still to a man / woman, the Republicans have been substantially better than the angry, hate-filled Democrats.

Donald Trump has a lot of Reagan toughness and goodness in him. He has a great plan for America and in this book, we answer definitively the question of one big supernatural reason "Why Trump Got Elected!" God picked him! God knew what Trump could do and he helped Trump's words reach all Americans so that those of us paying attention to God, could get him elected as our president.

Besides being favored by God, and maybe that alone was enough, Trump was and still is the best choice. Second, he is honest. Third, he has kept his word about making America great again in ways in which honest Americans are already pleased.

Trump is destined to be a great President. In my prayers I ask the Lord to take care of him so that he can provide for America for many years to come and set us up for another great leader when his eight-year mission is completed.

America has had more than one economic issue for sure, but it still is the best place to live on earth. When Donald Trump was inaugurated, our nation was full to the brim with economic woes. Now, tackled one by one, they are now being solved and right now, there are many works in process—all being solved thanks to our newest president.

This book reminds us of many of the problems that during the Obama years prevented many people in American from having a good life. Donald Trump and Mike Pence have taken on the mission to make life better for all Americans. God is on their side and our side in this effort.

Trump had a good life before becoming President. He did not have to help us. I am so glad he continues to work to make our country great again. I bet God whispered in Trump's ear to get him moving, putting all his gifts together to help America. Thank you, God. Thank you, Donald Trump.

I sure hope that all the readers enjoy this book and I hope that it inspires you to continue to take action on behalf of our country. Remember that Democrats hate God and they hate you. Read the Democrat playbook and you will find that God is bad; white people are bad; Western culture is bad, America is bad, etc., etc. Only Democrat power is good according to Hillary Clinton.

It is OK that their mob actions are not beneficial to Democrats. How can being against America and against God endear Democrats to the people? Being against our president; and against all of us cannot benefit America.

Our Congress in many ways is AWOL. They can certainly be more pro-American and more responsive to the people's needs and not their own. I hope the book in some ways helps you look at things differently.

Our new president has settled in and he is already implementing a host of innovative items on his agenda. I hope you digest Trump's entire plan, be willing to adopt it, and add to it your own positive notions for building a better America. And, please do not trust the press, CNN, MSNBC, or the NY Times, to do your thinking for you.

Together, we can help make the US a far better country. We should smile as we accomplished our first and best objective. With God's help, we elected Donald Trump as our president. Now, we must support his hard work and speak up to the Congress when they get in his way. Don't expect the Democrats to stop hating you, America, or God. Always be watchful for their next pack of lies.

Chapter 4 A Hero Given to America by God

I think God is a Trump supporter. I for one am very glad that he (Trump) came along. Aren't you?

Rep. Maxine Waters thinks God is on her side as she claimed the favor of the Almighty during a speech at a Capitol. It was a "Keep Families Together" rally in which she fired off the false charge that the President's policies separate illegal immigrant families. By the way, if you committed a crime and went to jail, do you think that your children should go to prison with you? Of course you will be separated.

Good ole Maxine, has little respect for the Lord. She said that Republican cabinet members and highly visible Trump enablers should expect harassment at restaurants, gas stations, shopping places, and even their homes until they change their immigration policy. Really? Then after calling all hell to be released on Republicans, she blamed Republicans for the terror bombs in the second last week in October. Amazing! There is no logic there at all.

Just because normal people and cabinet members living normal lies might not agree with Democrats, Maxine has sicced the mad mobs on them. As we know many have already been confronted at public places. It's getting scary out there. I can't see God calling for violence of any kind.

Unlike the messages God gives other politicians, He gives Trump a lot of leeway and a lot of great ammunition when fighting the enemies of goodness. Trump recently commented on Ms. Waters speech: "Congresswoman Maxine Waters, an extraordinarily low IQ person, has become, together with Nancy Pelosi, the Face of the Democrat Party. She has just called for harm to supporters, of which there are many, of the Make America Great Again movement. Be careful what you wish for Max!"

With the pipe bomb threat, Waters got her chance to rant again against President Trump. Waters blamed the President Trump for the bomb scare and demanded Trump "take responsibility for the kind of violence that we are seeing for the first time in different ways…"I think they are acting in a way that they think the president wants them to do and the way he wants them to act," Waters said of Trump supporters.

Funny how she stirred the pot; got a reaction; and blamed Trump for the reaction. Amazing! It is what it is. Her hate clouds her perception of reality.

That's enough for now. I think it would help for me to show you the email I sent out the other day to remind my friends and relatives about my perception of Mr. Trump before the election. It had been published pre-election in the local paper.

Only those who choose not to see, cannot see what is happening today with all the hate for God and Trump coming from and all the love from the right!. So, today I went back to the Wilkes-Barre Citizen's Voice Newspaper Archives and I found the letter to the editor that I sent to them two months before the 2016 election. I am glad God heard my prayer.

Perhaps you will enjoy this as much as I enjoyed writing it and rereading it. Those who stand still when they have the chance to act in God's favor often regret their inaction. I am tickled and proud that it being unpopular at the time, I was inspired to write this brief piece and send it in to the paper. If I could only open some hearts along the way, perhaps we could diffuse some of the hate that Democrats have for God and Donald Trump. After all, we are all Americans and thus we should all be for the best for America.

Here is what I sent: LETTER TO THE EDITOR / PUBLISHED: SEPTEMBER 11, 2016 WB CITIZENS Voice

There are many billionaires who want things their way on taxes and they figure they will benefit if their lobbyists get to the right politician. Donald Trump is actually running for office as a billionaire. He does not need a job. Yet, he is investing a lot of time in America. He does not need it. But, if he is successful, his kids will grow up in America and he wants it to be the finest country of any possible country ever. Bravo, Donald Trump.

Mr. Trump wants it to be like the America as founded by honest founders. Donald Trump is intrinsically honest. He may round up on some issues in his favor, but he is not corrupt. He wants his kids to love him and respect him just like you want your kids to think of you.

We are only on Earth for a short time. Why should we not do our best? I love that Donald Trump, a billionaire who needs me like a hole in the head, thinks I matter. He thinks you matter. He thinks America matters. He thinks God matters. He is right on all points. Unlike you and me, he has the means and the opportunity to really show God and his family what a good man he really is.

We have been waiting for you, Mr. Trump, since Ronald Reagan left us. God gave us Donald Trump. I am convinced that it is up to us to make him our president. We did not know how bad the Bushes were until they went into their recent crying tantrum because they lost. We just know that they were not too good when they had the power. Donald Trump is bombastic, arrogant when he knows he is right, and he is often inartful in his speech when he is upset. However, he, like my father, is a very good man. I welcome the opportunity to cast my vote for him. I thank God for the opportunity.

Brian W. Kelly

Chapter 5 Conservatives Are Mad as Hell from All the Hate.

I'm Mad as Hell!

Conservatives do not need a census to know that most reporters and editors are hateful, miserable liberal Democrats looking for a conservative to hate. There is a Pew Research Center poll out that found that liberals outnumber conservatives in the media by some 5 to 1, and that is lower than I would conclude from my own experience. Doesn't it get to you that almost every thought on TV, radio, and the social media is liberal and hateful and mostly always untrue.

However, for Democrat journalists, they think they should be excused because it is not their individual fault. When everyone else around you as you write the news is full of hate against God, country, or whitey, for a liberal, it is easy to be sucked into the chasm of group hate on what stories are important, what sources are legitimate and what the narrative of the day should be. For conservatives, whatever the progressive, corrupt Democrat media chooses to write is going to make us mad as hell. We can all be sure of that. Maybe if we saw a little truth every now and then, that might help.

The corrupt mainstream media has decided to be a branch of the leftist Democratic Party. It is hoping to succeed in its greatest potential act of pure hate. Its major mission is still to remove President Donald Trump from Office in any way possible and the quicker the better. Along the way the spreading of hate is both a mean and as a goal by itself. They don't really care whether America was or is great as long as nobody can credit God or Trump with making it great or greater or great again.

Fake news from CNN and MSNBC and the New York Times along with gratuitous lies, are the media weapons of choice and they have a huge following of lefty-type people, including Andrew Cuomo and his millennial followers. They enjoy the camaraderie of hate with the Governor, while they are enjoying their work of attempting to depose our duly elected president by hook or by crook.

Though most Americans are not privileged, the media and the Democratic leadership and a large part of the RINO Republican Establishment enjoy the fruits of political greed and the full benefits of all the hate within the "Swamp." It's been like that for too many years to expect that anything, the purpose of which is the good of the country, would have any meaning to them.

The daily soap opera of hate promulgated by this Democrat-controlled nasty press every day spews vile on the President and tries to convince weak-minded Americans that by playing against God, and jumping on their negative train, they can gain back the great times and the abundant power from the last eight great Obama years.

The press is actually worse than the far left in trying to persuade Americans to give up the Constitution and bring in a socialist regime that has no use for God.

Fixthisnation.com began their explanation for a new White House set of talking points intended to fight the fake news and it is the perfect way to continue this book about hate in and for America and how to ameliorate it. Why? Because like everything including the fake *Russia collusion soap opera*, the press tells one fat hate-filled lie after another.

MSNBC and CNN are the big culprits, but the disingenuous pedantic New York Times is not far behind in the lying category. So far, other than lefties, Americans are not buying what they are selling and that is good for the country.

"The White House often issues talking points to allies in the Republican Party– talking points that are almost certainly going to be ignored by politicians who refuse to stand up to the media's ideological tyranny. As far as the mainstream right is concerned, President Trump is completely toxic at this point and the hate for God is simply collateral damage. The *Mainstream right* is a new synonym for Never Trumpers and / or the SWAMP. Yes, Virginia, Republicans can be corrupt too if their purpose is to hurt Donald Trump in any way.

So, like rats from a sinking ship, Republicans of the "Never Trump" variety have done everything they can to distance themselves from the president, as if he really is the neo-Nazi, white supremacist that the liberal media insists that he is. Nonetheless the Trump faithful who love God and Trump, and who go to the rallies or watch the rallies, understand that the media cannot stop lying.

While smearing Trump, they hope to smear all of conservatism with the same racist brush. People who know people, love what Donald Trump is doing for America. Hate and Trump do not go together just like Hate and God are not compatible.

Just like God is the supreme being above all people, the President is the President of all America. However, the corrupt press and the Democrat Party have a mission to tell the people something else.

As Americans have begun to discern, the press is not only anti-Trump, they are anti-American, and ant-God, and they lie like the Devil, try to suck in weaker Americans, especially fragile millennials, into their doomsday party of hate. Many Americans simply can't take it anymore.

I can't take it anymore

Do you remember back in November 1976 when Howard Beale, as played by Peter Finch, the long-time anchor in the movie "Network News," gets the bad news that eventually causes him to utter one of the most famous movie lines of all time? Beale gets fired and is given two weeks. The long-time anchor has a very poor reaction to this personal news and he cannot control himself during the next broadcast. He "goes off the deep end."

He promises to commit suicide on the air. The company immediately fires him—no second chances for a repeat performance. Beale is devastated and remorseful. He begs for the opportunity to say good-by to his fans with dignity, and he is given his last opportunity ever for air time so that he can say his good-by's respectfully and also apologize. Nobody expects it to happen, but Beale gets his chance, and it is billed as a last chance.

Despite his promises, once on the air, Beale is overwhelmed by his circumstance. He goes into another diatribe starting off with a rant claiming that "Life is bullshit." He is so passionate that his ratings spike as he persuades his viewers to shout out of their windows: "I'm as mad as hell, and I'm not going to take this anymore!" Like the shot at Lexington and Concord, this is the line heard round the world.

Let that sink in, please. "I'm as mad as hell, and I'm not going to take this anymore!" We should all feel like that watching Democrat mobs run through their daily anti-American soap opera.

Well, my fellow Americans, I bet you saw this coming, and I am going to deliver it as passionately in words as I can: "I am mad as hell, and I am not going to take this anymore." I bet you are too. Let me remind you of why you are upset.

The hate today is at peak. Besides the CNN, MSNBC, New York Times and the Democrat Party hate for God and Trump, there are other issues that sour our citizens. Taxes are too high, elected officials are crooked and out of touch, government is too big, spending is out of control, the Obamacare program has been a train wreck from its inception, and heroes are dying in the VA system,

The people know that the federal government has been incompetent and for eight years, the left-wing news outlets purposely failed to report the truth about our corrupt and incompetent government. We the common citizens have had no voice in our own government before

Trump was elected; too many people are too lazy to hold government accountable, and too many of our finest local politicians are on the take.

Only you and I can bring this back to being OK, but not by sitting on our duffs and letting the hate mongers and fomenters win the day. We all need God's help.

A Train Wreck

Our country run by this government had been a train wreck and when they ran in 2016, Hillary Clinton, and Bernie Sanders promised to keep the train derailed for another eight years. They loved how things were. The people did not like it and that is why our President is now Donald J. Trump.

Trump put the train back on the tracks, but the Democrat Party as presented by CNN and MSNBC and the New York Times hate him for it and they would rather see a train wreck full of hate than a president saving America.

Corporate leaches and leakers full of hate for our duly elected President have infiltrated our government. We have record unemployment while illegal aliens are smiling as they take American jobs. We have an unsustainable status quo with special interests having priority over the people's interests.

When we look to the future we see a public education system that creates more dummies than smart people. These dummies are so dumb that they don't seem to mind being called dummies. Scrooge could have come up with an even more devastating term than "Bah Humbug." It's that bad! Can't you feel it?

Before Trump began putting us on the right track, we had the poorest economy since the depression with excessive welfare and income redistribution, institutionalized lying, a corrupt press carrying water for Democrats in government, a debt large enough to kill America, huge student debt stopping graduates' success, tyranny v. democracy, government lawlessness, freedom and liberty in jeopardy, American stagnation, and a big loss of American world prestige.

Why we do not regularly hear about this is because we have the most corrupt press since Gutenberg finally got his mechanical printing invention working. The American media in all forms works hard to propagandize all aspects of American life while championing the liberal leftist progressive wing of the Marxist / Communist oriented new Democratic Party.

Before Trump, our big government became such a problem that without a big change, it could never again be the solution. Yet the leftist press, rooting for a blue wave, wants to return to those bad days by ousting Trump from office simply because they hate him. They fear talking about the administration's accomplishments even though it should be the top news of the day. No wonder Trump and many others see their kind of news as "fake news."

Our finest hope, our youth; go through colleges with socialist / communist administrators and professors in huge numbers to ultimately become unemployed and sacked with debt. Why can't they get jobs? Illegal foreign nationals are given the jobs right out of college and graduate school because according to Democrats, white graduates already have it made. Really!

The out of touch hate-filled coffee-breath professors have convinced our mush-minded millennials that being unemployed is the new norm though their parents sent them to school because they believed that the American Dream was the norm. It was. But, no longer! Today's millennials do not believe in the American Dream or any dreams because their elitist professors hate America and they lecture accordingly.

The student loan burden prevents borrowers from buying homes, cars, and having a family. As many as 48 million student loan borrowers are too broke to engage in life. Coffee breath professors tell them that is OK. So what if they never will be well-to-do? College loans, instead of lifting people to the top, have created a new race to the bottom,

On the International stage, thanks to our elected government, America for the last eight years of Obama was known as a bad actor. Before Trump, nobody was giving America a standing ovation as our former president continually apologized for America's past.

Nobody was asking the US for curtain calls. Our leaders before Trump had turned their backs on our friends and they were paying homage to our enemies.

Nightclubs in Orlando created major carnage while, so as not to offend the new religion of acceptability in the US, the government blamed Christians and guns rather than the work of an ISIS terrorist, the hate mongering perpetrator of the atrocity.

A church is attacked by a deranged killer in Texas and Democrats don't want to hear that he lied about his dishonorable discharge and under current law should not have been permitted to buy any gun. Instead of hating conservatives and the second amendment, why would Democrats not try to treat people who are mentally ill?

Before Trump, smaller and weaker countries such as Russia, Iran, and North Korea pushed US around and laughed at US, and our only response was to see if somehow, we may have offended them. For me, these were the worst days of America that I have ever witnessed, and the leadership and our government at the time seemed to be OK with being mediocre, instead of being outstanding.

Our previously elected government had trained us not to fight the bad guys. Wimps and pure traitors from the Swamp still control the Congress and the Republicans may have won the last election but they fail to lead and to fulfill their promises to those who put them in office.

If you have been paying attention, and I sure hope you have been as it is a civic duty, you know that there are even more issues than the exhaustive list we just walked through. Isn't that a shame on US? I think that is why you bought this book. Thank you very much. We do not have to be filled with such hate, but we must recognize its existence.

We are on the same side, and together we can all help. We must not be quiet. Instead we must talk about all the hate spewed by Democrat Mobs all the time. It is unhealthy.

The hate mongers win when America is quiet about the issues. People should not be afraid to discuss any topic in the US—ever. Know that as of today it is OK to talk politics at family dinners unless we are ready to give our country to those who hate us and would do us harm.

We first must understand what is going on and we then must understand our rights. God is good regardless of what Democrats tell you. Trump has a great record regardless of what the corrupt media tells you

Mad as hell

Before you and me and everybody else are on board with fighting Democrat hate and lies, we must start the first wave of solutions by opening our windows all the way and shouting as loud as we can—just like Howard Beale—so all of the government perpetrators in Washington can hear us well: "I am mad as hell, and I am not going to take this anymore."

Then, we must make sure that we talk to everybody we can out there that we know—other people like you and I and others, and let's help them know that unless we all fully engaged in America, when we wake up from our deep fog, there may be no America left for our progeny.

We will have blown it for sure. We must try every day to get those that harbor so much hate for our God and our President and for America to stop the hate and begin again to love their fellow man. Love America!

We should watch the movie *Network News* again and especially Howard Beale's antics for a refreshed perspective on hate. Howard Beale was a fictional character 40 years ago, but 40 years before Beale there was a real figure named Adolf Hitler who likewise stirred a nation to anger and insanity. He eventually dragged the whole world into a World War. Adolf Hitler's end was tragic, as was the end for Howard Beale. I don't know about you, but I am still mad as hell about all the hate!

Chapter 6 Democrats Hate America, Trump, God, & Lots More!

Don't expect help from Democrats

Many normal Americans and even politicians are waking up and coming to the conclusion that Democrats Hate America. They also hate Trump; and they Hate God.

Rick Saccone, PA-18 GOP nominee spoke up and made comments about his opinion of modern Democrats at one of his recent campaign rallies. He was a political candidate in the Spring 2008 but failed in both bids.

Besides Saccone, more and more Americans are concluding that the Democrats either hate everything in the world that is not Democrat or they are pretty good fakers.

Saccone made his opinion well-known at a rally at a local volunteer fire department in Blaine Hill, PA. He later squared off in March against Democrat Conor Lamb in the special election for Pennsylvania's 18th District, before the mandated PA redistricting.

Prior to the early 2018 special election, Saccone is quoted in a video posted to Twitter by NBC News saying: "They say the other side is energized, Let me tell you, they're energized for hate for our president.

They have a hatred for our president. I've talked to so many of these on the left, and they have a hatred for our president. And I tell you, many of them have a hatred for our country."

"I'll tell you some more—my wife and I saw it again today: They have a hatred for God," Saccone said. "It's amazing. You see it when I'm talking to them. It's disturbing to me." Mr. Saccone, it is disturbing to me also as well as most America-loving and God-loving Americans. I know the good people of America will make the power-hungry Democrat poor losers pay for that in the next election. All Americans see what is going on.

I am at a loss to be able to say how a Democrat can win any election today. I know many Democrats and the only way they are going for what clearly is bully mob-rule is because they actually don't believe what is in their own faces. America would be better without a Democrat Party.

<< Here is a picture of Saccone and his wife greeting President Donald J Trump.

Conor Lamb, a Democrat, pulled off an extremely narrow but major upset in PA by winning a special House election in the heart of Pennsylvania Trump country. Mr. Lamb won in the state's 18th Congressional District, a reliably Republican seat in recent elections and an area that Donald J. Trump won by nearly 20 percentage points in 2016.

The victory some think, was an ominous sign for Republicans ahead of this year's midterm elections. However, Lamb won by just .02 percentage points, so Republicans have not begun to collectively hold their breaths.

Some conservatives like to paint the Democratic Party as being hostile to religion because they are. The Republican House candidate Rick Saccone, who lost his race to Lamb for Pennsylvania's 18th District, spoke his mind on the Democrats. It did not help him in the special election, but people remember. As 2018 moved closer to the election, the Democrats nasty behavior on all fronts gave all citizens a closer look at their radical mobs.

DEMOCRATS

AMERICA'S OLDEST HATE GROUP

THEY STARTED & SUSTAINED THE KKK
CREATED & ENFORCED "JIMCROW" LAWS

ARRESTED MARTIN LUTHER KING
OPPOSED CIVIL RIGHTS
OPPOSED & FOUGHT AGAINST
THE RIGHT FOR AMERICAN BLACKS TO VOTE

DON'T YOU THINK IT IS TIME FOR
AMERICANS TO GET OFF
THE DEMOCRAT PLANTATION
& THINK FOR YOURSELF?

Conservatives have observed this negative and mostly outlandish Democrat behavior for years and have thirsted over those years for a more muscular and unapologetic conservatism and for the bright light of truth to be directed onto these darkest habits of modern leftists.

When the regular people spoke in 2016, the election of Donald Trump began to propel us down a road featuring satisfying helpings of both. America got to see the full regalia on a stunning day, September 27, 2018. One-time milk-toast Republicans arose in resolve like nothing in recent memory. The accompanying reputational suicide of several key Democrats tied a bow around a historic day for a clarity showing just what these people are and what they stand for.

Almost everybody in the country, friend and foe observed the occasion with shock and alarm. It was not that long ago that the totally unnecessary session of testimony by Supreme Court nominee Brett Kavanaugh and his main accuser of sexual misbehavior, Dr. Christine Blasey Ford was front and center in the news.

The occasion was needless because Dr. Ford's story in no way rose to the level of credibility to dislodge the nomination. No decent society smears people for life based on high school misbehavior, so even if the wholly unsupported story were true, there would have been a strong argument against its relevancy today.

Nonetheless, there we were, a nation bathed in the splendor of TV screens for a day that began with Dr. Ford's compelling testimony. However, the poised delivery of her story in no way increased its credibility. Only corroborating evidence can do that, and none arose to bolster her claim of a sexual assault at Kavanaugh's hands.

For Kavanaugh's part, he knew he was being railroaded by unscrupulous Democrat Senators as did most of the nation. He sat down with a bolder, more resolved countenance than we saw on his understated Fox News interview.

Flashing a similar irritation, reminiscent of Clarence Thomas's 1991 excoriation of the Senate Judiciary Committee, Kavanaugh delivered an opening statement that doubled down on his already established denials, expanding to include special disfavor for the discredited tales woven by a New Yorker article and showboat attorney Michael Avenatti.

We do not have to relive it in this book. Almost every American looked at it with the sense of repugnance for Democrats that it deserved.

Townhall.com explained how it went from the opening bell of the afternoon session when Kavanaugh got to say his piece.

"As soon as Judge Kavanaugh completed his opening statement, it became clear what the afternoon matinee would contain: Republicans showing more spine than they have in years, accompanied by Democrats making total asses—of themselves."
…
"The confirmation of Kavanaugh [became] … a moral necessity—so that a good man's reputation [could] … be restored, rules of basic decency upheld, and viciously craven political tactics [by Democrats] dealt the death blow they deserved."   'Nuff said!

Tough running for office with little funding

Back to the Saccone comments, I know how difficult it is to win a national election with minimal funding. I ran for the US House myself in PA in 2010 with a miniscule campaign budget. The press said I did well with 17% of the vote in the primary. I was a babe in the woods.

Saccone was not a babe in the woods but he was more a regular guy than a politico and so he lost to the well-financed Democrat by .02%. He did lots better than I did.

The Republicans had a better candidate to endorse in the primary election cycle though Saccone is a good man. In 2018, Guy Rescenthaler sought the Republican nomination for Pennsylvania's newly redistricted 14th congressional district. He defeated Rick Saccone in May 2018 by a small amount to win the Republican Party's nomination for PA District 14.

Though Saccone was vocal in his condemnation of Democrats in the special election period, it was not an issue in the primary between two Republicans. However, you can bet that whether they are saying it or not, Republicans know how far down Democrats have sunken in trying to regain power.

The characterization of leftists as hostile to faith obviously didn't start with Saccone . It has been around for years. We all have seen televangelist Pat Robertson, a Christian Right pioneer. He famously said: "Just like what Nazi Germany did to the Jews, so liberal America is now doing to the evangelical Christians. It's no different. It is the same thing. It is happening all over again. It is the Democrat Congress, the liberal-based media and the [immoral fringe groups] who want to destroy the Christians."

According to the Pew Research Center, a group that studies such matters, they say that self-identified atheists are more likely to be aligned with the Democratic Party and with political liberalism. Pew found nearly 7 in 10 — 69 percent — of atheists are Democrats or Democrat-leaning, and more than half — 56 percent — call themselves political liberals. It is hard to find a falsehood in Saccone's comments.

If we generalize the comments—that the left hates God, they are no truer than the idea that the right, the party that most white evangelicals align with, loves God. Whether it helps politically or not, it is true. More and more brave political candidates are finally seeing the light and making such assertions.

Meanwhile Democrats are busy hating Trump, God, and the United States of America. What do they expect to gain?

Chapter 7 Thank You Mr. President

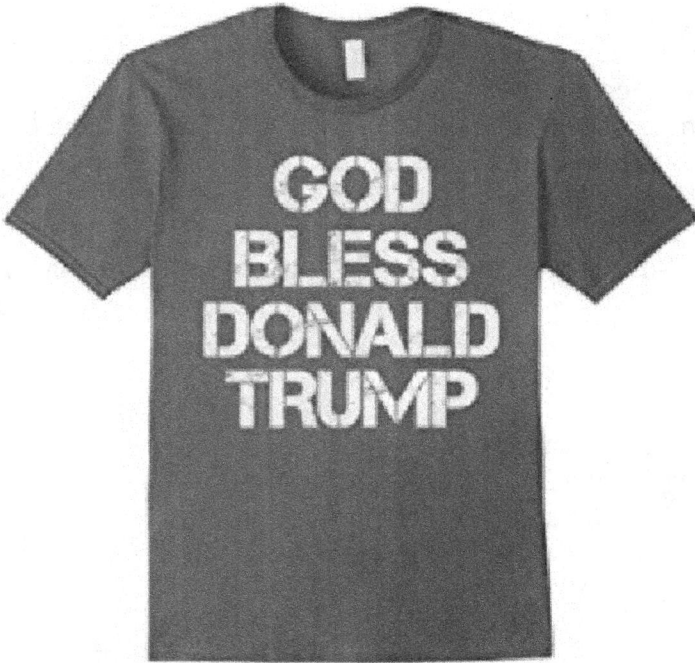

Dear Mr. President

Besides God saying it would be like that, there were a lot of reasons why you became President # 45. Mr. Trump. You and your team pulled off a whale of a victory. I only wish I could have voted more than once, but then again, it was not needed. Moreover, I am not registered in California. It was perfect how you and your team pulled off his victory. It is tough to differentiate direct intervention from the gifts God gave to "The Donald" at birth. Either way, you have been blessed by God to deliver a fresh new country to the people.

Why did God give us Donald Trump? Well, it is logical that God, who knows all things, knew that you were His best answer. Democrats in their quest for power may choose to hate God but you know that nobody in their right mind can deny that God has more power than the Democrats. President Trump, please continue to remember that

Love or hate?

You either loved Donald Trump when he ran for President or you
hated him. There was no in-between then and there is no in-between
now. I have seen a number of conversions but I also see too many hard-
nosed democrats willing to give up their faith for the Democratic Party.
It is hard to believe. Like Jesus on the Cross, I ask God to *"Forgive them
Father for they know not what they do!"*

If you love America, even if you may have trusted Obama, with no
good reason, few were ready for four more Obama years with Hillary
Clinton as his new name. God protected us by sending Donald Trump
as his personal emissary.

If you never figured that out, or if you are now flirting with the new
Winfrey on the block to become the popular president then I regret that
you, my friend, are a part of the problem, not the solution. It is a
problem that America and Americans must solve before this country
can ever be great again on a consistent basis.

Trump and God got us here, but can Americans handle the success?
Will we throw it away on the Winfrey du jour in the future? Say "No!"

Can you imagine how successful the anti-American deep state would
have been with Mrs. Clinton as president? I thank God, every time I
realize that Donald Trump is the President of my United States of
America.

I can't wait to hear the Oprah's first post-racial address. Since Obama,
everything is about race? It is because Democrats have stopped dealing
with real American issues such as jobs, and real healthcare for the
working class.

After a full year and almost a full second year, I still happen to love our
President for the right reasons. As I have noted many times, I find him
to be a gift from God to the American people in our time of great need.

After all the weak, wimpy, wobbly conservative leaders, groomed by
establishment elitism, who offered little recognition or solutions for the

concerns of the American citizens for many years, it all chenged in 2016.

Donald J. Trump, my candidate for president, and the candidate of most Americans, has been a deep breath of fresh air. Among the Republican electorate, his approval rating is a chart-topping 88%. Hey, I approve, and I am a reluctant Democrat.

Thank you, Donald J. Trump for doing the United States a big favor by taking on corruption in both political parties as well as the media. You are doing just fine and my friends and relatives appreciate your taking a hiatus from your wonderful storybook life and using your time to help us. We sure need it.

Supporters cheer as President Donald Trump speaks in Great Falls, Mont., on July 5. Among Republicans, his job approval rating stands at 88%. PHOTO: JOSHUA ROBERTS/REUTERS

Though some felt when you ran in 2016 that you were not a viable candidate at the beginning, I was not among their ranks. I saw you grow from day one, when you were introduced to the piranha at the first Republican primary debate. You did very well but nobody, especially Meghan Kelly of Fox, would acknowledge you because you were and continue to be the biggest threat to all of the establishment elites in both parties. You are especially not liked by the corrupt press because you call them out on their dishonesty. Thank you, President Trump.

You have taken the Republican electorate by storm (88%) and I love watching you climb higher and higher in the polls, though when you ran for office, Hillary Clinton. was always deemed to be the favorite by the corrupt media. On your way to a great victory, you also won over many Democrats including a number in my own family—long time progressives who had finally had enough of liberal lies.

I am sure you have heard that many switched to Republican, so they could vote for you in the PA primary. They are all very smart people, especially my wonderful sister-in-law, Diane who never gave an inch before Trump. She became a Trumpster. It took a while for a lot of Democrats, such as I, to know that today's Democratic leaders are really progressives who care little about the American people and that includes most regular Democrats.

Buried in the 12% disapproval rating are some real conservatives, nationalists, and populists who believed that the elite Republicans who later were identified as the SWAMP and the NEVER-Trumpers could never be trusted.

Some, like the Bushes, we had once trusted enough to give them governorships and even presidencies—did not serve us well. So, God helped us recently understand that the Bushes were always for the elite and they all but lied to the people about important American issues such as immigration. We did not know the real answer then but wondered why there was no action that benefitted American workers on immigration in eight Bush years. We know now.

What a disappointment for me and many. The whining Bushes became babies about your rough way of dealing with them as political foes. They are now Never-Trumpers of the highest order, meaning they have no regard for the American people who voted for them and they have no regard for you, President Trump. I lost my respect for the Bushes when they exchanged their love of America for selfish retribution. I look at them as low-life Democrats.

Along with a number of one-time favorites of conservatives, these guys had always been against conservatives but had lied and played along for political gain. I have a list of some of the most notorious of these "outlaws," without mentioning the Bushes again but I will spare you the pain of reciting their names.

Many, who still hold elected office have gotten quiet or have recanted their negative allegiance. You have more than proven yourself already so I know these scalawags don't phase you.

You know that many have come back but many still reject your platform and thus they reject the will of the people. For self-preservation, many quietly came back into the fold. However, there are many more, such as those in the list which I have, who have not come back, and many have become Democrats or DINOs to spite you. Why the Democratic Party would even want such people is a conundrum.

But, then again to be a Party means you must have followers. Any Party that hates God deserves all the Never-Trumpers it can find.

Chapter 8 God is Good! He Cares About All of His Flock.

ESPN's GameDay was at its ever best

Some find it distasteful that anybody, including your author, would suggest that Democrats hate God, even though when queried, the same people would admit that it sure does not seem like Democrats have much if any love for God or religion. I happen to love God and I also love the idea of God and I am not bragging. I am just saying. I am reminded of our loving God all the time, especially on October 20 watching the Purdue Boilermakers v the # 2 ranked Ohio Buckeyes on ESPN

We have already discussed that many Democrats are atheists and that most atheists have a built-in hate for God. It is part of the nature of being atheist. We also discussed that since Republicans are known to be followers of religion and God, and Democrats hate Republicans by definition, and Republicans credit God with their success, which of course comes out of the hide of Democrats, it follows that on this count, Democrats have a big reason to hate God. Few analysts other than those who enjoy begging the argument could argue with a straight face, however that Democrats do not, indeed, hate God.

In the last ten years, the idea of Democrats being for the people and for great values has diminished substantially. Consequently, when a Christian discovers that a particular family or a particular individual consistently supports and/or votes for Democrat candidates, they are given a label or are considered not a true-blue believer? Why is this?

Well, it is easy as you look at what Democrats say they are all about. So, the reason we may think this way is that Democrats tend to believe in abortion (killing babies), and they seemingly are against believers, or at least the rights of believers. Another reason is Democrats like big government and are for making people dependent on Government.

So, many think Democrats are purposely destroying America. Additionally, Democrats provide no soothing solutions about the ability of the Christian faith to survive. Christians are not blind. Not everyone in the Republican Party is a saint, and of course, not all those in the Democratic Party are sinners.

For another reason, we can go back to scripture. Ephesians 5:15-16 warns us to "Be very careful, then, how you live—not as unwise but as wise, making the most of every opportunity, because the days are evil." We know the days are not good as we wake up in today's world.

In many Christian circles, it is believed that God is removing his hand of protection over the nation due to sin. Yet, there are many Christian leaders who see God's hand in bringing Donald Trump, a rogue perhaps, but a God-fearing rogue to America to help us all.

Pew Research studies this issue all the time. In their research, they discovered in recent times that half of Americans who have left their church no longer believe in God. This has led to a surge of nearly one quarter of the nation who have no affiliation with any religion, according to one of their newer surveys.

The Pew Research Center sees that 49 percent of what they term "nones" (not Catholic, Protestant, or Jewish) left their church and religion because they "don't believe." Another 20 percent said they don't like organized religion. Other reasons included "common sense" and a lack of belief in miracles.

The survey is the latest from Pew that demonstrates a growing trend in America. More and more people are junking religion and many are giving up on God. In this survey they did not peg all of the fallout on Democrats, but we know that the Evangelicals and Republicans in general are more religious even without Pew telling us so.

I think that even among those who do not believe in miracles, they would like to believe especially with loved ones involved. Unless they were simply carrying anger on their sleeves, many would like miracles to be real and would not deny a miracle if they encountered one. Democrats would be tougher to convince than Republicans for sure .

I believe in God and I do believe in miracles and like many of both ideologies, I have prayed for miracles numerous times in my life. Most often these prayers are regarding the illness of a loved one or dear friend or a person who captures my heart.

God loves Tyler Trent. He was able to make the big game on Saturday

Tyler Trent loves God and the Purdue Boilermakers Football Team. Tyler received a number of miracles over the past wekend proving again that God is love and deserves no hate. Gameday highlighted the recent life of Tyler Trent in a completely non-political football expose on Saturday Morning October 20.

Every Saturday Morning for the last several years, I have looked forward to watching GameDay a program that attracts more and more fans, mostly students from the home university every week. You may recognize these names from seeing these pro announcers sitting at the big table every Saturday Morning at 9:00 AM EDT.

- ✓ Kirk Herbstreit
- ✓ Lee Corso
- ✓ Desmond Howard
- ✓ Tom Rinaldi
- ✓ Rece Davis
- ✓ Gene Wojciechowski
- ✓ Maria Taylor

On this particular Saturday when the Boilermakers of Perdue were playing the Buckeyes of Ohio State at Ross–Ade Stadium on the campus of Perdue University, something big was in the air. The GameDay crew put on a segment that was so heart-moving, I felt my eyes watering long before it was even half-over.

One of the Purdue Boilermakers' greatest fans, Purdue sophomore Tyler Trent was 18 years old, when diagnosed with bone cancer twice. His story captivated millions during the ESPN Oct 20 Saturday College GameDay and it hit a high note later in the evening to a nationwide audience . Tyler Trent's Boilermakers upset previously-unbeaten and second-ranked Ohio State. I would call it a miracle from God. God brings miracles when even Democrats do not expect them.

Five Purdue Captains crowd Tyler Trent with Nebraska Game Ball

The GameDay feature showed Tyler when he was very healthy and then they showed what has happened since the cancers. You could see in the younger (before) pictures of Tyler that were shown in the segment that Tyler was a normal young boy who, in his own handsomeness, looked healthy as a horse. Nobody would have ever expected what eventually became his health legacy.

While the GameDay cameras were rolling, this young man described that he knew what he faced. He shared with everybody that in his earliest battle, he had simply taken a normal Frisbee in a normal family fun day, and he winged a good one. However, he got such pain that he had to be hospitalized. His winning throw caused enough body trauma to him that it was enough to break his arm. It was not expected. No childhood cancer is expected. It would melt anybody at any age to hear such a story. It was time for a miracle. He got his miracle

Tyler had a major operation that medical professionals were hoping would arrest the disease. It did. For two years Tyler was back to normal hoping to never face cancer again. Surgeons took out his diseased cancer riddled broken bone in his upper arm. They replaced his humerus (upper arm bone) with a Titanium prosthetic implant. On the show, they showed an X-ray. The lower bones remained intact while the Titanium artifical humerus lit up the X-Ray. Prosthetics involve the use of artificial limbs (prostheses) to enhance the function and lifestyle of persons with limb loss.

Unfortunately, a positive prognosis is not a declaration of continued wellness. Tyler's family along with Tyler were given the bad news after he was cancer-free for about two-years. The bone cancer had spread to his spine. As noted, Tyler Trent was diagnosed with bone cancer twice by age 18. He's had nine major surgeries in the past three years. The **_Purdue University_** sophomore and die-hard sports fanatic is determined to live life on his own terms, come what may. He is now battling cancer a third time and this is a tough one.

Tyler Trent is a Boilermaker. Let that forever be enshrined in your mind. Watching the Purdue v OSU game on Oct 20, was inspirational knowing Tyler Trent, who was iffy about being healthy enough to make the game. Was at the game. The entire home crowd was aware of Tyler and they were rooting for him as much as he was rooting for them and their mutual Boilermakers.

Yes, on this Saturday night, at kickoff of the Purdue Boilermakers' **_big upset against No. 2 Ohio State,_** the Boilers' home crowd collectively did a chant to honor a very special young man: Tyler Trent, a Purdue student and diehard Boilermaker fan who has terminal cancer. Picture a stadium full of fans as excited as this. How could the team not have responded with a victory for Tyler and God?

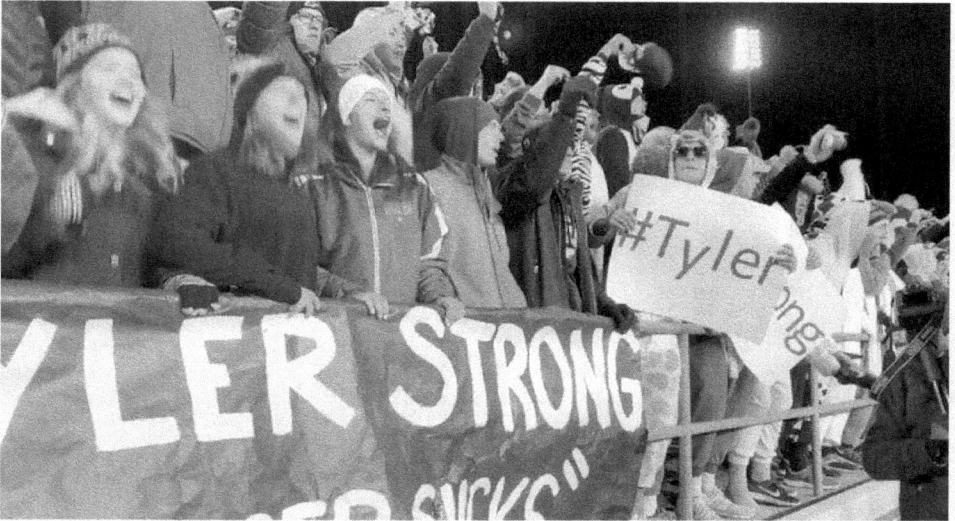

In the segment we saw on Gameday, mom and dad and other family as well as what appeared to be the entire 2018 Purdue Football team (Five of Eight Captains) before the Ohio State game circled around Tyler's bed. He had become aware that ESPN was going to view this special piece on its Gameday on Oct 20. This tweet and the subsequent conversation gives us all an idea of what type of person Tyler is:

Tyler Trent ✔
@theTylerTrent

update: I'm sad to say I will not be making it back to #Purdue. 💔 My health has taken a turn for the worse and the level of care I now need is too great. While I may not know how many days I have left, I'm trusting the one who does! #onlythestrong #boilerforlife #godsgotthis

6:09 PM - Sep 29, 2018

♡ 8,277 ◯ 1,036 people are talking about this

Here is a bit of a "conversation Tyler had with Mike Carmin from Jouran & Courier, part of the USA Network:

Here's more of my [Mike Carmin's] conversion with Trent:

Question: Do you want to talk about your situation and where you're at right now?

Answer: Right now, I'm at home under the care of my parents and Riley (Hospital for Children). We're just seeing how things go. Hopefully, Lord willing I'll be at the Ohio State-Purdue game (Oct. 20) and cheering Purdue on but I'm not planning on returning to school anytime soon, that's for sure.

Q: What have doctors told you about your prognosis?

A: Prognosis right now is like hospice and what you would expect from hospice. Sitting and waiting type of thing. The Lord takes you when the Lord takes you. The cancer has spread to a point where it's untreatable and that's OK and I'm OK with that. That's where things stand.

The head coach of Purdue is Jeff Brohm, the 36th head coach in program history. He is a very impressive human being and Tyler is one of his guys. The Boilermakers compete in the Big Ten Conference as a member of the West Division. Interviewed after the game, Brohm offered how much the team cares for Tyler Trent.

The team and the locals got Tyler Press-Box seats for the big October 20 game, so that he could see Ohio State v Purdue at home at the stadium. Nobody, including family knew whether he would be strong enough to be lifted into a carrier that would be strong enough to transport him into the stadium. Many of the details of how Tyler got to the game were kept a secret until we saw him smiling in the Press Box window.

There were no more secrets left when the Game Day camera crew snuck a bunch of photos through the clear windows of where Tyler was watching the game. He looked like he could have been one of the coaches.

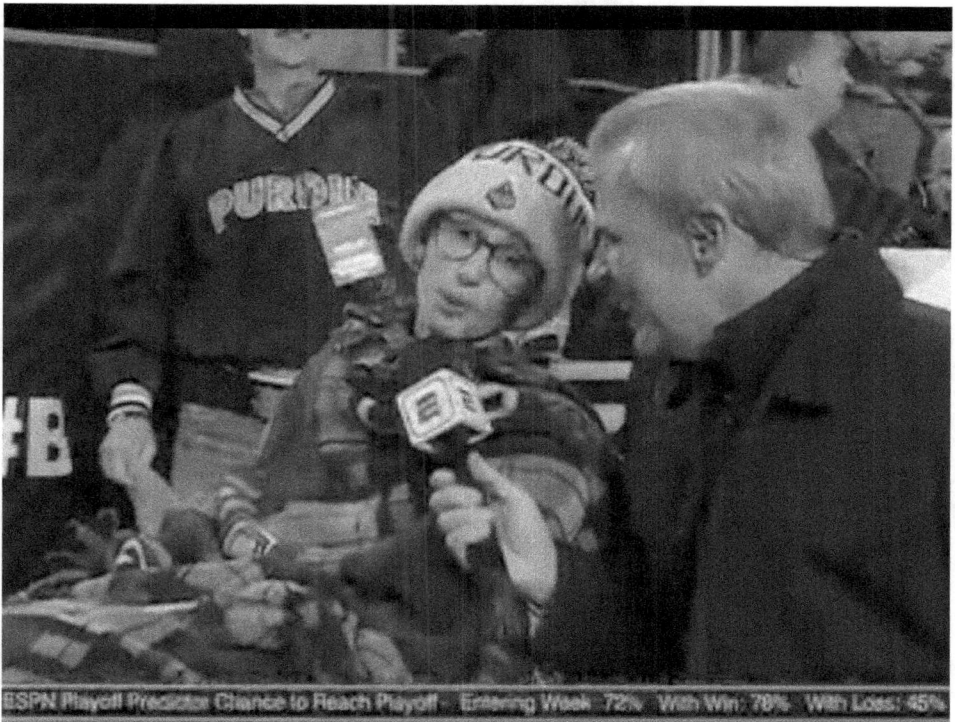

Pic taken when Tyler came onto the field on his way to the locker room

During the Game Day special program that aired on Saturday morning, Tyler was seen in his bed looking feeble and weak. He received the game ball from the Nebraska win from the players. He was encircled by five of eight captains from the Purdue Football Team with star QB David Blough right next to him on the bed. My wife Pat and I were more than overjoyed to see a strong, bright eyed Tyler Trent emerge before the game ended.

His family got him down to field level on the sidelines with Purdue at the time, near the end of a shellacking of Ohio State. The sophomore, battling cancer every day, looked more like a Football Analyst than a patient as he was interviewed on the sidelines by Tom Rinaldi above. The topic at the time was the huge Purdue lead and Tyler was offering his thoughts on his continued belief in a Purdue win. It was inspiring, especially after Purdue took a huge lead over Ohio State courtesy of D.J. Knox., David Blough, and company.

Tyler had been invited to the Purdue Locker Room for a win or lose celebration. He was stopped momentarily for the Rinaldi interview.

You just gotta love Purdue and its people. Soon afterwards, time ran out with OSU in possession of the ball. On the way out of the stadium, all the fans seemed to have relocated to the playing surface of the field to celebrate the victory with Tyler et al.

Purdue head coach Jeff Brohm was able to find just a small amount of space on the packed field to chat with Maria Taylor about his team's win over Ohio State. He made a point about the inspiration his team gets from Tyler Trent. On this great day in Indiana, it was a mutual experience. It showed clearly the power of God.

Gregg Doyel of the Indianapolis Star wrote a great column the day after the game played in West Lafayette, Indiana on the Purdue campus:

> The miracle wasn't what was happening on the field, though what was happening on the field was rather remarkable: Purdue was beating No. 2 Ohio State, beating up the Buckeyes, moving all over the field and getting into the end zone and denying Ohio State the same privilege. This was a Purdue team that began the season with three consecutive losses, and the Boilermakers blew out the undefeated and No. 2 Buckeyes, the scoreboard showing a 49-20 victory as tens of thousands of Purdue fans swarmed the field, covering it from sideline to sideline, from end zone to end zone.

> That wasn't the miracle. Games never are, you know? But people are miraculous, and what was happening in a suite high above the field at Ross-Ade Stadium was something along those lines. It was a Purdue student named Tyler Trent, a young man from Carmel, a sophomore who has battled cancer and battled it and battled it — and here he was, at this stadium, in this suite, making a return to campus that doctors said couldn't happen. He withdrew from classes this semester to come home, where he is in hospice care, refusing to give cancer what it has come several times to take from him.

> "Had to be here," Tyler is telling me before kickoff, though that's not the last time I saw him Saturday night. After the third quarter, with Purdue leading 21-6 — before D.J. Knox busted a 42-yard touchdown run to make it 28-6 — I'm leaving the press box for the

suite level, where the Purdue pep band has come to play the fight song outside Purdue President Mitch Daniels' suite. One door down is Tyler, in the Purdue University Center for Cancer Research's suite. Daniels had spent time Saturday night with Tyler as well, because Tyler is the magnet attracting the rest of us like steel shavings, and after the third quarter Tyler is sitting in his wheelchair, in his gaudy Purdue blazer, overlooking the field. Tyler is sitting next to his father, Tony, and he is beaming.

"Told you," is what Tyler tells me, and he's right, he did. He has been telling anyone who would listen that Purdue would win this game, which is why he had to be here, even as his kidneys are failing him and the nephrostomy tubes placed in his kidneys are failing him — the tubes leaked several times this week, sending him to the hospital — and weeks ago he lost the use of one arm and both legs.

How Tyler made it to this suite, well, that's a story. Condensed version: A Carmel police escort led the family out of their neighborhood, past the stone column with the yellow "Tyler Strong" ribbon on it, past the neighbors who were standing on the side of the road, cheering Tyler toward what could be his final trip to Purdue. In the car with them is a secret service agent, the kind that protects the president and vice president, an agent who had come from West Lafayette to ride with the family. With a wave of a credential, the agent got them through busy checkpoints near the stadium, which attracted its biggest crowd in five years.

How does a secret service agent end up in Tyler Trent's car? Well, the secret service was at Purdue anyway Saturday, doing some training with local officials, but also this happened a few weeks ago:

Tyler's cellphone rings. He doesn't recognize the number, but he's been getting calls and visits from all sorts of new friends. Purdue football coach Jeff Brohm has been here, and Colts kicker Adam Vinatieri, and even Tom Rinaldi and the ESPN GameDay crew, which aired a feature on Tyler earlier Saturday.

Tyler answers the phone.

"Tyler?" says the voice on the other end. "It's Mike."

Mike who, Tyler asks.

"Mike Pence."

It's been like that.

Tyler Trent's fight with cancer has captivated all of his campus, much of the state and even parts of the country, and Saturday night was something that everyone who loves Tyler Trent — that list is long, and I'm on it — wanted to see happen:

We wanted Tyler at this game. And, yes, we wanted Purdue to win it. For Tyler, you understand? Win it for Tyler. Which is what Purdue's captains had told him they would try to do a few weeks ago when they visited him at his home, bringing the game ball from their victory at Nebraska.

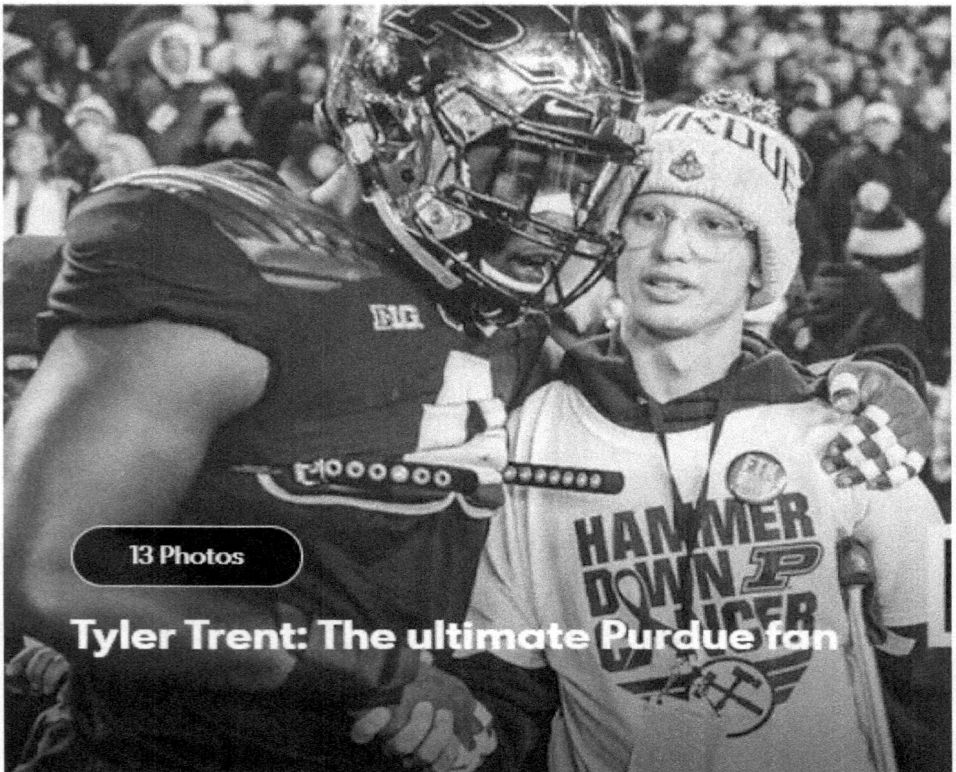

13 Photos

Tyler Trent: The ultimate Purdue fan

Being Catholic, and from Pennsylvania, My wife Pat and I have been Notre Dame and Penn State fans since the pablum days . I had told Pat earlier in the day how moved I was by the ESPN GameDay segment featuring Tyler Trent.

Pat became very interested in the Ohio State v Purdue game and even more interested in seeing Tyler Trent make the game to have his wish come true. She and I are both Boilermaker fans as of Oct 20, 2018, even though we have loved Indiana for a long time before Oct 20, by being ND fans.

Notre Dame had a bye and Penn State had just eked out a win v Indiana University. That's a lot of Indiana for one day for sure. We watched this game with even more interest than if the Fighting Irish were playing OSU instead of the Boilermakers.

We could see that even in a weakened condition from his bout with cancer, Tyler Trent is one tough kid at 20 years old. If he had the wellness and the physical stamina, he's the kind of young man that would be the best player on the Boilermakers' team. He says he is a Boilermaker. The Purdue Coach says he is a Boilermaker; and from everybody's perspective. he sure is a great Boilermaker.

He took off this past semester to get well, but in the Gameday segment, his mom told the world his prognosis now is terminal. Pat and I are hoping it is stopped at a bus terminal in life, waiting for reinforcements.

Some call people like us fools but we never rule out anything as God has all the power and he uses it as he chooses, not as we choose. So, no prayer for Tyler is wasted.

With that big smile of his, he convinced the Lord God almighty to listen to his plea. It was more than enough that he had bragged expecting a big Purdue win over OSU, 49-20. So, I would not have expected him so soon to brag again by predicting his next big victory would be against Cancer. But, I wish it were so.

The way I see it, if God was willing to give Tyler and the other Boilermakers a 49-20 win v Ohio State, with his relationship with God, I would not rule out a private conversation in which God gave Tyler some other very good news. God is the Lord and Master.

Tylor is part Bionic

You may already know that Titanium is a special element used for
bone replacement. It is a strong element from nature and it makes the
body think that a prosthesis is not a foreign object so that the body will
not reject the artificial part. My titanium knee for example has served
me well since 2010.

After two glorious years with an upper arm made of Titanium, Tyler
and his family got the bad news. His cancer was back; and it did not
look good though the young Trent had been fighting it as well as any
person ever had or could.

Tyler always loved the Purdue Boilermakers Football team and he saw
as many games as anybody his age during his well-time. Taylor has his
own way of dealing with bad news.

That ESPN GameDay segment on Saturday Morning 10/20/2018, was
as good a presentation of an issue and a story as anything like that—
that I had ever seen on TV—ever. It got to me and to many and we are
all praying for Tyler.

It was obvious that all of Purdue University, including the football
team, the band, the head coach, all the other coaches and quite frankly
everybody in West Lafayette, and the rest of Indiana, were looking at
Tyler as a very special inspiring person. With that came a mutual
admiration society, and I mean that in the nicest of ways.

The committed Purdue football fanatic, Tyler Trent, regardless of his
recent setback and being cared for by Hospice, continues to be
determined to live life on his own terms despite his terminal diagnosis.

Tyler Trent not only has the support of his family and friends, but as
you can see, he also has the support of the Boilermakers football team,
the Boilermakers fan base, and the full student body. Tyler supports
them all back.

That is a lot of prayers from a lot of people. Nobody knows God's
plans; but anybody who follows God knows that the Lord surely
granted Tyler a miracle on October 20 to help keep his smile where

God wanted it. His game prediction came true and his wish came through.

It does not take a cleric to see that God's signature was on this miracle for Tyler Trent as Purdue, a "getting better" 3-3 team at the time, not only defeated the # 2 team in the nation, Ohio State, but they more than doubled the OSU point production by a whopper score of 49-20. Whew!

Purdue led the whole game, but a slim lead is not enough against Ohio State. Penn State learned that just a few weeks ago. So, even without ever relinquishing the lead, the game was tense as the lead v OSU was slim. Slim, that is until D. J. Knox heard God's calling and he more than listened to the spirit that moves all the chess-pieces of life.

We all admired Knox's moves as he cut through the tough OSU defense. OSU may never had played a team in which the Lord himself was wearing the opposition team's uniform.

Purdue's D.J. Knox ran for 128 yards and three touchdowns while QB David Blough threw for three more scores and the Boilermakers held Ohio State's vaunted passing game in check most of the night. The Boilermakers turned up the heat on the Boiler and erupted for a 49-20 upset to shake up the College Football Playoff chase.

While getting ready for a nice night's sleep, Pat and I found ourselves biting down hard on our teeth, hoping for the best but knowing how powerful Ohio State is and how easily they have come back to dethrone champions.

So, every time my wife Pat and I blinked waiting for the next play, it seemed D.J. Knox was making somebody miss a tackle; heading for a narrow escape; and then running with a full head of steam towards pay dirt. And, then *whew*, crossing the goal line. How sweet it is when the team that you are rooting for seems to be rooting for you!

Looking at game stats, clearly all of the major go-ahead was in the second half and despite OSU coming alive, Purdue never lost any life.

The Purdue fans became calm when in his third break-away, Knox finally made everybody, including Tyler Trent feel comfortable with the lead. It wasn't until it was almost the end of the game that Urban Myer was not trying to win. He has a lot of tricks in his bag and nobody took OSU for granted even with a big Purdue lead.

Purdue fans, actually believed that "we" were going to win the game. God knew right from the start that this would be a "W," and so did Tyler Trent. We knew that the determination and skill of Urban Myer might take it away and that is why it was tense until there was no more time.

With Tyler Trent, a Boilermaker himself, cheering on the rest of the Boilermakers, nobody can deny that this day and this game was a real miracle. Now that Purdue has beaten Ohio State, we all know that God never sleeps. It would be wonderful if the Lord of Heaven and Earth eventually chooses to cure Tyler.

We all pray for that beginning but we realize God has his own plan for Tyler. I am inclined to believe that Tyler knows God's plan and he is OK with it. In all cases, we pray for what is best for Tyler.

Sometimes the miracles that God delivers are big and sometimes they are not as big. On Saturday, Oct 20, and I am not kidding you, I witnessed a miracle. It depends on whether you are a Purdue Boilermaker as to whether the miracle was a real big one or not.

For OSU, it was definitely a nightmare. It certainly was unexpected for everybody but Tyler Trent. The circumstances of this miracle indicate that the hand of God was involved 100% in this miracle. Ask Tyler Trent.

When talking to Tyler who knows everything about himself, and perhaps everything in West La Fayette, Ind. and perhaps everything on the Purdue Campus, and I am not kidding, you can ask Tyler Trent how he's holding up. Tough question for a guy dealing with cancer. Though just 20-years old, he does not flinch. Tyler is well aware of the big stakes. He is well aware of his own circumstance; but he is a tough Boilermaker for sure.

"I'm doing fantastic, thanks for asking," Trent said after the Nebraska game from his home in Carmel. He is always upbeat. He is always optimistic. He is always humble.

Once I was a confirmed Tyler Trent supporter, after witnessing GameDay live. I picked up all of my Tyler Trent information in a short period of research. My wife got most of hers from me. Tyler Trent is contagious as I believe he would like to help make God.

I never saw my wonderful wife Pat as excited about the outcome of a football game as the OSU v Purdue game on this particular Saturday Night. Tyler Trent got his football wish and he made us all feel well after his interview. He looked great for all of his ordeals and the Boilermakers gave their favorite Boilermaker fan his greatest Boilermaker gift – a huge victory over Ohio State. His story is the perfect addition to this book.

There is no greater force in the universe than God. On Saturday, Oct 20, though there was no cure for Tyler Trent on the horizon, and that clearly would have been the bigger miracle of the day, there was definitely a miracle. It was the one asked for by Tyler Trent for himself but also for others. The Boilermakers defeated the Buckeyes and for most of us, other than the Buckeyes, that is a sweet sound.

It positively affected a young man who one day may be asking the Lord for a cure. But, on this day, Tyler Trent thanked God for granting a big wish. OSU went home losers v Purdue's Boilermakers.

Tyler's wish being granted affected a whole nation looking for good news. Though I am sorry that OSU had to take it on the chin for Purdue to win, they are a fine team and they took it well. That made Tyler Trent's victory and miracle real.

Let me end with this notion. God is good; God loves Democrats and Republicans alike . God gives tough people tough medicine like he gave to Tyler Trent. God knows that Tyler will be with him for eternity.

Everybody, including my beautiful wife Pat and I, who became associated with Tyler through his love, has already climbed higher on the pearly ladder thanks to the young Trent, That, of course will be even more meaningful when we all see God as our friend on a regular basis.

I wrote this quote down from my research, but I do not know who said it. I will add an attribution as soon as I know who it was who gave me this great quote.

Regardless, here is what they said and we should all pay attention:

"There are moments in life when you witness someone who transcends their existence, bringing hope and encouragement to those affected by similar debilitating circumstances. Purdue fan and former student Tyler Trent, a 20-year-old stricken with terminal bone cancer, is proof of this."

As Tiny Tim would say:

God bless us, everyone!

Chapter 9 Democrats Led Our Nation Away from God, etc.

The Inconvenient Truth About the Democratic Party

Democrats are responsible for lots of bad things

More and more good people are looking at the world we live in and concluding that the new Democrats are responsible for a lot of bad stuff. In June 2018, the Editor of the News Register made some profound observations and conclusions in his piece titled:

"Democrats Led Our Nation Away From God ."

Check out the Internet and you will find many similar thoughts:
*http://www.theintelligencer.net/opinion/letters-to-the-*editor/2018/06/democrats-led-our-nation-away-from-god/

Editor, News-Register:

America has betrayed our founders!

America has betrayed our God!

Christians escaped religious persecution in Europe and with God's divine intervention, created our great nation. Ten-plus miracles by God sustained our founders during our Revolutionary War. Perhaps if Democrats review these miracles they will not hate God so much.

The US forces were outnumbered 10 to 1 by a well-trained and disciplined British army, but by God's grace we won! It was an amazing miracle.

Miracles persisted throughout the war. George Washington led in battle, often within 50 yards of the British! He had four bullet holes in his coat and two horses shot from under him. He did not get a scratch. Praise God! George Washington read his Bible daily. Does God love America? You bet!

An enormous British armada gathered in Boston Harbor and prepared to level the city with canon fire. Bostonians prayed and fasted. That night, a huge storm blew the armada out to sea and sunk it. Far more battle miracles occurred, to be found with a little research.

God loves America today and has loved US from the beginning. Only recently have Democrats introduced themselves to their progressive ideology. Democrats see progressivism as the replacement god for the real God. For progressives and Democrats, the state is their god and the real God has no role. They do not miss God at all. They loathe Him.

Despite Democrats taking issue with the notion that the US is a Christian nation, it nonetheless is true. From 1775 to 1783, our Continental Congress issued 15 proclamations. Without exception, each humbly beseeched Almighty God's hand in their endeavors. Our founders held church services. Most of the early 13 states had a state religion. Only Christians were permitted to hold public office. America was certainly born a very Christian nation. Have you ever heard of a Christian Terrorist?

Our First Amendment prevailed over many court challenges over many years, setting much early legal precedent. America coexisted with God for well over 150 years … until 1947. In 1947, against all court precedent, against the Constitution of the United States, nine Democrat Supreme Court justices declared separation of church and state. America became a secularist nation — a government without God.

This created a new court precedent for the incremental moral decline of America. It has been declining since. Only the people who remember keep God alive. This precedent became the Democrats' ploy for America's trip to hell. They ignored American heritage in pursuit of their agenda! They found progressivism with Woodrow Wilson and then believed they needed no God but the state.

In 1952, the Lyndon Johnson amendment forbade pastors to speak politics in the pulpit, separation of church and state allowed Democrats to take prayer out of school. The high school pregnancy rate doubled in 10 years! In 1973, Democrats passed Roe v. Wade, allowing the murder of babies in the womb. Democrats then took Bibles out of hotels.

Democrats removed the Ten Commandments from the courthouse in Montgomery, Ala., We know from recent attacks at Christmas time, the display of religion on public property is under constant attack by Democrats. This is not by all government officials folks. This is an attack by God-hating Democrats who have the same disdain for Jesus Christ, His only Son as for God Himself.

A Democrat Supreme Court s legalized same-sex marriage in 2015. No matter where you are on the issue, the US never took a stance on the notion of a "GAY" lifestyle but the Sacrament of Marriage was a sacrament for many.

A Democrat president expelled God from our military. He also gave us same-sex bathrooms in 2015! Today, Democrat judges penalize Christians who choose to follow their religion rather than abide by recent rulings.

The reign and the rain of secularism over three generations destroyed our weakest American families. Lack of the Judeo-Christian ethic has exacerbated divorce, school shootings, riots, rape, unwed mothers, gangs, etc. We had no school shootings until secularism eroded our culture. Think about it. There are those who see no linkage. Think about it.

Though we no longer see "God is Dead," on the news, quietly Democrats have incorporated the belief that God is unnecessary by weaving it into their progressive ideology. Our secularist culture is the catalyst for school shootings.

Democrats, not Republicans, have created our secularist society and they are sustained by less informed voters. The Democrat Party has betrayed our Founding Fathers! The Democrat Party has betrayed God! The Democrat Party hates God. Who can offer proof otherwise?

No matter how great a person that others believe you to be, your parents, who may have passed-on years ago, more than likely in today's environment of godlessness, would suggest that you hold your faith. They would not ask you to become complicit in the hate of God.

Some of us who examine what is really what believe that if you, good as you may feel about yourself, opt to vote with the godless Democrat Party, who are you? You and others like you who hate God in the name of progressivism and the Democratic Party are the reason things are the way they are. Why else? Can America be better when you choose to be the same?

Yes, though you do not want to face it, to vote Democrat makes you complicit in this US travesty. The party of slavery is now the party of abortion. Jesus would not support their evil, anti-God agenda. Jesus loves you but he hates your sin! Jesus Christ would not vote Democrat! How can you vote Democrat and call yourself Christian? Share Jesus to save America for our children and grandchildren.

Don Krahel of St. Clairsville was the primary author of the above piece, though your author adopted it for Fall 2018. The Krahel piece was titled *Democrats led our nation away from God*. Krahel is a good person. He cautions those who believe in God that FaceBook is one of the instruments from HELL that Democrats are using to finish off their work of taking God out of the United States once and for all. He would say that "Facebook is not your friend if you are a friend of God."

Remember, Democrats led our nation away from God

DonKrahel Productions shared a photo.
October 19 at 12:18 AM · 🌐

Facebook is trying to get folks to remove this picture from their profiles because it is "offensive". Let's band together and prove them otherwise!!!!!

If you are a Democrat and you want to be an even better soldier for the progressive movement and the Democrat cause, just fire your hate for God up a few more notches and you may get your wish.

WHY DO LIBERALS HATE GOD?

Exclusive: Joseph Farah explains vitriolic reaction to Ten Commandments campaign

Joseph Farah, founder WND.com

The notion of Democrats being at odds with God, to put it mildly is not new in 2018 though it is more obvious than ever. Joseph Farah from World Net Daily, way back in 2013 asked a simple question as the title of an article. The title tells of the problem liberals have had with God for many years.

His premise is very accurate. Liberals really do hate God. It is a generalization because no survey was taken. Not all liberals hate God, however. But the visible evidence shows overwhelmingly that liberals, as demonstrated by history and of course today's Democrat Party reject God's attributes—His authority, His reality, and His Truth.

Farah reveals in his piece that he has known that God has been missing from liberal thought for a long time, but the idea is strengthened, rather than softened as time passes. The behavior of Democrats clearly misses the moderating touch of a Supreme Being.

Looking for some comments on the Farah article, I found a gentleman named Bill Montane who said :   *There are a ton of Vile people out there. There are too many (shouldn't be any) Swamp Critters in politics. And we know ALL the Democrats are corrupt. Remember though, it comes down to*

WHO counts the votes. Can we trust them? Does Soros still own the voting machines? God help us!

Even Rush Limbaugh makes an occasional comment such as a dire prediction about what happens if Democrats win the house. *"They're off the rails. I pray they lose both houses again. They'll ALL be rioting in the streets and calling for civil war."*

Franklin Graham found something truthful to say about Farah's piece:

> *What has happened to the Democrats? God has turned them all over to their own craziness. It all started when they decided to make the killing of babies their number one issue. How crazy do you have to be to support the stabbing of little ones in their necks? Good grief. Think about it this way. If a mother walked up to you on the street and told you that she would give you $300 to take her baby and rip it's head off. Would you do it? Well the Democrat party supports baby killing so much that they honor and protect the murderer abortionists who slaughter babies for money. This is why the Democrats have gone crazy.*

Here is a comment from my buddy Andy G:

Hi Brian, Democrats hate GOD because HE knows what is in their hearts. That is why GOD has placed them on the LEFT, with Republicans on the RIGHT. Andy G.

Democrats are becoming all they claim to hate

https://www.commentarymagazine.com/politics-ideas/liberals-democrats/democratic-party-lost-mind-mimic-gop/
APRIL 4, 2017
BY NOAH ROTHMAN

Noah Rothman's thesis in his essay below offers additional insights:

The Democratic Party's strategic incoherence is a risky gamble.

It is clear now that Democrats learned all their worst lessons from their perception of the conduct of their political opponents over the course of the Obama presidency. Obama was the worst of the worst presidents.

However, Republicans held their cool and did not become nutsies and God haters as the Democrats have since Trump emerged victorious in 2017. If the truth be told, I bet it would indict Democrats for hating their very own selves. But, Democrats also hate the truth.

With unchecked bitterness, Democrats convinced themselves that the right side of the political spectrum did little more than obstruct, distract, and indulge their basest impulses for eight years.

For this, and no other apparent reasons, according to Democrats, the Republicans were rewarded with total control of all the levers of government in Washington when Mr. Trump took the oath in 2017. The Nut-House Ambulance should have been called to take all Democrats for treatment. If they were treated in 2017, it would not necessarily be so bad today in 2018.

Thus, anticipating rewards for nothing, Democrats immediately embraced a policy of strategic incoherence with no grander objective than mollifying their base. Their technique was simply to irritate the duly elected president . In the process, they have become the very creatures they once claimed to oppose.

"Donald Trump, you didn't win this election!" declared new Democratic National Committee Chairman, Tom Perez. Perhaps anticipating that his explicit contention that Donald Trump is an illegitimate president would yield some uncomfortable parallels, Perez preemptively defended himself. "I don't care," he said, "because they don't give a s— about people."

That's some defense! But it is all they got!.

The Democrat rallying cry that Donald Trump has no right to the office he presently occupies is an argument that hardly merits much attention. It consists entirely of the contention that he didn't really win states that no Republican presidential candidate has won in almost 30 years—Pennsylvania, Michigan, and Wisconsin

Why did Trump win. The faux real Democrat rationale is that
Russian intervention into the election might have changed how
voters intended to cast their ballots. Cut me a break, please. Does it
not make you want to throw up in disbelief that Democrats are
such sore losers?

Democrats embarked on one self-destructive maneuver after
another as their base became disgusted and sang historically
significant songs such as "Is that all there is!" Hey, that's all there
was in this dishonest world.

Democrat leadership has given regular Democrats nothing but hate
for anything not spelled D-E-M-O-C-R-A-T. Since God did not
pass the Democrat spell check, He too had to go. But many
Democrats left the fold when that was all there was.

Many wonder who the Democrat base voters could be when the
mainstream press claimed they had been forced by their base to
perform a futile, ill-fated gesture of defiance in the face of
overwhelming odds—not in spite of those odds but because of
them.

Without help from the folks in white coats, it is obvious that
Democrats have gone nuts. In the grassroots, demand of their
representatives for a display of conviction and the will to oppose
Donald Trump's agenda at every turn and no matter how long,
have helped make their Party meaningless and unimportant to
those who understand reality.

The irony is that the Democrats' lack of an achievable strategic
objective is precisely what they criticized the GOP for during the
better part of six years. As a Democrat, I concluded long ago that
there is no Democrat Party. It's gone. They are gone. As a
Democrat myself, at first, I wondered. Now, I wonder if anybody
knows what time it is. Does anybody care?

While Democrats flirt with the inane and the insane, Republicans
have gotten rewarded with more electoral victories, more policy
concessions from Democrats, and more power.

Can it be that Republicans have become victims of their own success in winning elections while Democrats were self-exploding and becoming prisoners of their own failures. Ironically, a great mind would easily find that the caricature of Republicans as painted for years by Democrats now is revered by the Democrats so much so that they are mimicking the cartoon of the GOP that exists in their minds.

Democrats are now convinced that they do not have to display moderation or even basic cogency or decency to win back the power they lost in the Obama years. Some think they might be right, but there are loonies everywhere. They are off the rails wrong.

Supporters of the Party of D know that if they are wrong, and if the tactically foolish sacrifices of authority and credibility they're making today do not pay off, they'll find themselves at the bottom of an abyss.

It can easily be argued that abyss is an even more cynical and embittered place than where God-hating Democrats are in today. And with a more radicalized base nursing a sense of betrayal, the Democrat Party's time in the wilderness may last a while but eventually, those who love America will wake up and simply get rid of the Democrat Party.

They're nuts! They hate other Americans. They hate the world. They hate Trump, and worse than any of that, they hate God. Democrats have no chance. Abandon Ship!

Noah Rothman wrote the base article for this analysis by your book author.

Noah Rothman
Noah Rothman is the Associate Editor of *Commentary*.

Chapter 10 Thank You God for #CLUELESS Democrats

Thank You God for #CLUELESS Democrats

By Wayne Allyn Root

https://townhall.com/columnists/wayneallynroot/2018/07/09/thank
-you-god-for-clueless-democrats-n2498428

The reason that I included the entire piece written by Wayne Allyn Root is because it belongs in this book about the hate Democrats have for God Almighty.

Before I understood who Franklin D. Roosevelt was, other than the 32nd President of the USA and the only President ever elected for four terms, I knew my dad believed that Roosevelt saved regular people during the great depression. My father always had something good to say about Roosevelt.

As more and more Democrats came and went, my dad, who had convinced me to join the Democrat Party after I spent two years as an

Independent, no longer believed Democrats offered the same honest promise as he believed Roosevelt had offered to Americans.

As his children became old enough to survive even if my dad lost his job, my father took a different look at the forces that control our country. He was never anti-Democrat but he looked at each presidential candidate as a man with ideas, not a man representing a Party with ideas. There is a big difference. I know of peers whose parents taught them *Democrat or nothing*. Not my dad.

We grew up with a big radio in the living room, which we called the Parlor and we listened to it intensely. Boston Blackie, The Lone Ranger, and The Shadow, were my favorites but until 1956 when we got a 1957 Admiral TV on "time," all we ever had were the great voices from that huge radio in the corner. Nobody knew what anybody in the distance called stardom ever looked like. Then we turned on the TV.

After offering me one choice in 1971 about being an Independent or a Democrat, I changed from Independent to Democrat so I could vote in the PA Primary. As an independent thinker, as time went by my dad and I voted the same often. We both, for example, loved President Reagan and he got our vote.

We both began to look at Democrats with skepticism because they tried to overwhelm the typically uneducated with what dad and I would call, Bullsh-t. It was just that and so we began to look funny at Democrat promises and their charges that Republicans were bad, bad, bad.

My point is that though I had no interest in politics, I had a major interest in our country. My dad and I talked about the issues each election and we voted accordingly. We were not tethered to the Democrat Party. Over time, our votes for R were far more than our votes for D because the R's had a better game plan to help America than the Democrats.

Today, the progeny of long-term Democrats are bullied into adopting all the crap that Democrats choose to deliver, which if sold as food would be inedible. I have a tough time reaching these peers who learned the wrong way from their parents. Every now and then something like a Trump comes along which pushes more of these

people out of the Democrat Party. So, think of that as my introduction
to the idea of clueless Democrats because I know many still exist.

Wayne Allyn Root is a nationally syndicated conservative TV and
radio host known as "the Capitalist Evangelist" and "the
conservative warrior." He is a CEO, business owner, business
speaker, conservative media commentator and best-selling
conservative author of "Angry White Male" "Murder of the Middle
Class" "The Ultimate Obama Survival Guide" and "The Power of
RELENTLESS!" Wayne is creator and executive producer of
many hit reality TV series in Hollywood. He is host of "WAR
Now: The Wayne Allyn Root Show" at

www.USAradio.com and www.NewsmaxTV.com

For more, visit his website: www.ROOTforAmerica.com. Follow
him on Twitter@WayneRoot.

Wayne Allyn Root is one of a few who have been publicized as
being classmates of President Obama at Columbia though he does
not recall meeting him. ROOT: *Well, I'm sure I did. I just never knew
him. We were both political science majors at the same college, Columbia
University, graduated in the class of '83. So I guarantee you we were sitting
in the same classes together but I did not know him. It's probably a
graduating class of 600 or 700. So it's very possible to be in the same class
and not know a person. I didn't know everyone in the whole class.*

Wayne Allyn Root

Posted: Jul 09, 2018 12:01 AM

The Democrat Party is #CLUELESS.

The Democrats probably weren't going to beat Trump anyways, or the GOP, no matter what they did, or said in either November 2018, or 2020. The economy is just too good. But they certainly had a chance, if they didn't go completely off the rails.

But then they chose illegal immigration as their headline issue. Really? And as their new star (DNC Chair Tom Perez calls her "the future of the party") Dems just elected Alexandria Ocasio-Cortez, a proud Socialist. She was a bartender last year, now call her "Congresswoman." She believes in open borders, abolishing ICE, sanctuary cities, and get this one- "Illegal aliens deserve the right of passage to freely enter the USA." Her words. I'm not joking.

No one could be that dumb and clueless, could they? Yup. See "DEMOCRAT" in the dictionary.

I'll get to all that. But first the good news coming in waves for President Trump.

*The Trump economy added another 213,000 jobs in June. The Labor Dept also revised April and May's jobs figures upward by 37,000 jobs.

*Even better news- 601,000 Americans re-entered the workforce in June. The economy is so good, wages are rising so fast, everyone on the sidelines wants back in the game.

*A record 155,576,000 Americans were employed in June, the most in history.

*Pay growth is up every month this year, with blue-collar wages growing the fastest.

*Because of Trump's "Hire American" policy, even disabled Americans are seeing record job growth.

*The U.S. trade deficit just plunged the most in 10 years! And US exports rose to an all-time record. Trump is winning the "trade wars" for American workers and companies.

*As wages and savings rose, Americans spent less on utilities. Why? Over 100 electric, gas and water utilities have saved $3 billion with the Trump tax cuts.

*Because of the Trump tax cuts over $300 billion was repatriated to the US in just the first quarter- the most money in history ever brought back to the USA.

How bad can it get for those poor, poor, clueless, delusional Democrats?

In their infinite wisdom (because we all know how intellectual they are- or at least that's what they keep reminding us), Democrats have chosen illegal immigration as their main issue for the upcoming election. And Alexandria Ocasio-Cortez as their poster gal.

Did I mention that Ocasio-Cortez is a proud Socialist?

Did I mention in addition to open borders and abolishing ICE, she believes in free college for all, free Medicare for all, universal income (everyone gets a salary from government for not working) and get this, she thinks everyone who wants a government job should be provided one. I'm sure she'd give a plum government job (plus lifetime pension) to every MS-13 gangbanger who asks nicely!

That's your platform? Really? You're not kidding? Democrats must believe in assisted suicide.

The latest polls from Summer 2018…

*A majority of blacks & Hispanics want stricter immigration laws.

*Only 25% of voters want to abolish ICE vs 55% who support ICE.

*Americans are united in opposition to Sanctuary cities- with 84% of voters wanting illegal aliens turned over to authorities.

*50% of American voters favor changing to a merit-based immigration system vs. 34% who prefer the existing family-based system.

*Trump's approval rating is up 10 points one month with Hispanics.

*Reuters reports young white Americans are fleeing the Democrat Party in record numbers. Overall among all young voters, Republicans are now amazingly tied 39-39 with Democrats. Yes, among young voters.

If I wrote this storyline in a movie script, not one liberal Hollywood movie mogul would buy it. They'd say it's too far-fetched. They'd say no one could be this blind, deaf, dumb or clueless. Yet the Democrats are actually doing this in real life. It's stranger than fiction.

Trump was elected to secure the border, build the wall, strengthen ICE, deport illegal criminals, end Sanctuary cities and by doing all of this, create millions of high-wage jobs for Americans.

He's doing it all. And it's all working. And out of all the issues, Democrats want to take it to Trump on this issue [Immigration] [Hey, are the members of that huge "caravan" aka invasion force that is headed our way being fed and watered and porta pottied by kind Democrats who hate America and hate God?. The invasion cannot be supported by regular Democrats because there are none left. They have been gone since the "Worker's Party" days of their parents. Now Democrats are the party of lost causes—they of course are the causes of losers]

Thank you God, for the gift of #CLUELESS DEMOCRATS.

From Wayne Allyn Root –

Thank you from the book author, Mr. Root for your great contribution to this book

Epilogue

In this chapter, we borrowed from Wayne Allyn Root, who offered a cogent set of reasons about how Democrats have *exited stage left* and all those who did not bail, have gone off the deep end.

This essay by Wayne Allyn Root did not add much to the ongoing story about Why Democrats Hate God. They do what they do, according to Root and many others because they are clueless about good and evil as well as the notion of God and no-God. They hate America, Americans that love America, white males, God, and anybody else who gets in the way of their power quest.

Hate is their answer to everything. It's just that it actually answers nothing and proves that though they come off vindictive and nasty to all, which is their goal, they are clueless for sure

I suspect that since you held out until the last word to turn in your reading glasses, that you have been reading. Thank you.

I began this book with a premise that some choose not to accept. **Democrats hate God.** That is the premise.

So, instead of *Do Democrats Hate God* as the title, it became *Why Democrats Hate God?* Since much of the hate shown by Democrats is visibly towards President Trump, the feelings of Democrats towards the President was a natural inclusion in this book.

Since the position of many people who love God is that God sent Donald Trump to save the people of America, and Democrats hate Trump because he beat a Democrat, that was enough for Democrats to hate God. Worse than that if you are a Democrat is that Trump is actually saving the people of America. Democrats cannot accept Trump success.

Democrats finally realized while wallowing in their intense hate for Trump, that because God loved Trump, they had to hate the God who sent Trump to dethrone the Democratic Party.

Democrats hate God

How can they not hate God when He in all his goodness wants them to reject all of the nasty precepts of the Democrat Party itself.

Before Democrats even realized they hated God, they noticed that the Lord God loves Donald J. Trump. They had no choice at this point but to hate God.

They must have forgotten that God is the Supreme Being and when even Democrats die God decides where they spend their eternity.

Bye Bye Miss American Pie.

My advice to the party of D is "Smarten Up!" There is only one God and like it or not, you have P-ssed him off big time.

.

Other Books by Brian W. Kelly: (amazon.com, and Kindle)

No Tree! No Toys! No Toot Toot! Heartwarming story. Christmas disappeared while 19 month old was napping
How to End DACA, Sanctuary Cities, & Resident Illegal Aliens . best solution to wipe shadows in America.
Government Must Stop Ripping Off Seniors' Social Security!: Hey buddy, seniors can no longer spare a dime?
Special Report: Solving America's Student Debt Crisis!: The only real solution to the $1.52 Trillion debt
How to End DACA, Sanctuary Cities, & Resident Illegal Aliens . best solution to wipe shadows in America.
The Winning Political Platform for America A unique winning approach to solve the big problems in America.
Lou Barletta v Bob Casey for US Senate Barletta has a unique approach to solving the big problems in America.
John Chrin v Matt Cartwright for Congress Chrin has a unique approach to solving big problems in America.
The Cure for Hate !!! Can the cure be any worse than this disease that is crippling America?
Andrew Cuomo's Time to Go? "He Was Never that Great!": Cuomo says America never that great
White People Are Bad! Bad! Bad! Whoever thought a popular slogan in 2018 would be It's OK to be White!
The Fake News Media Is Also Corrupt !!!: Fake press / media today is not worthy to be 4th Estate.
God Gave US Donald Trump? Trump was sent from God as the people's answer
Millennials Say America Was "Never That Great": Too many pleased days of political chumps not over!
White People Are Bad! Bad! Bad! In 2018, too many people find race as a non-equalizer.
It's Time for The John Doe Party… Don't you think? By By Elephants.
Great Players in Florida Gators Football… Tim Tebow and a ton of other great players
Great Coaches in Florida Gators Football… The best coaches in Gator history.
The Constitution by Hamilton, Jefferson, Madison, et al. The Real Constitution
The Constitution Companion. Will help you learn and understand the Constitution
Great Coaches in Clemson Football The best Clemson Coaches right to Dabo Swinney
Great Players in Clemson Football The best Clemson players in history
Winning Back America. America's been stolen and can be won back completely
The Founding of America… Great book to pick up a lot of great facts
Defeating America's Career Politicians. The scoundrels need to go.
Midnight Mass by Jack Lammers… You remember what it was like Great story
The Bike by Jack Lammers… Great heartwarming Story by Jack
Wipe Out All Student Loan Debt--Now! Watch the economy go boom!
No Free Lunch Pay Back Welfare! Why not pay it back?
Deport All Millennials Now!!! Why they deserve to be deported and/or saved
DELETE the EPA, Please! The worst decisions to hurt America
Taxation Without Representation 4th Edition Should we throw the TEA overboard again?
Four Great Political Essays by Thomas Dawson
Top Ten Political Books for 2018… Cliffnotes Version of 10 Political Books
Top Six Patriotic Books for 2018… Cliffnotes version of 6 Patriotic Boosk
Why Trump Got Elected!.. It's great to hear about a great milestone in America!
The Day the Free Press Died. Corrupt Press Lives on!
Solved (Immigration) The best solutions for 2018
Solved II (Obamacare, Social Security, Student Debt) Check it out; They're solved.
Great Moments in Pittsburgh Steelers Football... Six Super Bowls and more.
Great Players in Pittsburgh Steelers Football ,,,Chuck Noll, Bill Cowher, Mike Tomin, etc.
Great Coaches in New England Patriots Football,,, Bill Belichick the one and only plus others
Great Players in New England Patriots Football… Tom Brady, Drew Bledsoe et al.
Great Coaches in Philadelphia Eagles Football..Andy Reid, Doug Pederson & Lots more
Great Players in Philadelphia Eagles Football Great players such as Sonny Jurgenson
Great Coaches in Syracuse Football All the greats including Ben Schwartzwalder
Great Players in Syracuse Football. Highlights best players such as Jim Brown & Donovan McNabb
Millennials are People Too !!! Give US millennials help to live American Dream
Brian Kelly for the United States Senate from PA: Fresh Face for US Senate
The Candidate's Bible. Don't pray for your campaign without this bible
Rush Limbaugh's Platform for Americans… Rush will love it
Sean Hannity's Platform for Americans… Sean will love it
Donald Trump's New Platform for Americans. Make Trump unbeatable in 2020
Tariffs Are Good for America! One of the best tools a president can have
Great Coaches in Pittsburgh Steelers Football Sixteen of the best coaches ever to coach in pro football.
Great Moments in New England Patriots Football Great football moments from Boston to New England
Great Moments in Philadelphia Eagles Football. The best from the Eagles from the beginning of football.
Great Moments in Syracuse Football The great moments, coaches & players in Syracuse Football
Boost Social Security Now! Hey Buddy Can You Spare a Dime?
The Birth of American Football. From the first college game in 1869 to the last Super Bowl
Obamacare: A One-Line Repeal Congress must get this done.
A Wilkes-Barre Christmas Story A wonderful town makes Christmas all the better

A Boy, A Bike, A Train, and a Christmas Miracle A Christmas story that will melt your heart
Pay-to-Go   America-First Immigration Fix
Legalizing Illegal Aliens Via Resident Visas Americans-first plan saves $Trillions. Learn how!
60 Million Illegal Aliens in America!!! A simple, America-first solution.
The Bill of Rights By Founder James Madison Refresh *your knowledge of the specific rights for all*
Great Players in Army Football Great Army Football played by great players..
Great Coaches in Army Football Army's coaches are all great.
Great Moments in Army Football Army Football at its best.
Great Moments in Florida Gators Football Gators Football from the start. This is the book.
Great Moments in Clemson Football CU Football at its best. This is the book.
Great Moments in Florida Gators Football Gators Football from the start. This is the book.
The Constitution Companion. A Guide to Reading and Comprehending the Constitution
The Constitution by Hamilton, Jefferson, & Madison – Big type and in English
PATERNO: The Dark Days After Win # 409. Sky began to fall within days of win # 409.
JoePa 409 Victories: Say No More! Winningest Division I-A football coach ever
American College Football: The Beginning From before day one football was played.
Great Coaches in Alabama Football Challenging the coaches of every other program!
Great Coaches in Penn State Football the Best Coaches in PSU's football program
Great Players in Penn State Football The best players in PSU's football program
Great Players in Notre Dame Football The best players in ND's football program
Great Coaches in Notre Dame Football The best coaches in any football program
Great Players in Alabama Football from Quarterbacks to offensive Linemen Greats!
Great Moments in Alabama Football AU Football from the start. This is the book.
Great Moments in Penn State Football PSU Football, start--games, coaches, players,
Great Moments in Notre Dame Football ND Football, start, games, coaches, players
Cross Country with the Parents A great trip from East Coast to West with the kids
Seniors, Social Security & the Minimum Wage. Things seniors need to know.
How to Write Your First Book and Publish It with CreateSpace. You too can be an author.
The US Immigration Fix--It's all in here. Finally, an answer.
I had a Dream IBM Could be #1 Again The title is self-explanatory
WineDiets.Com Presents The Wine Diet Learn how to lose weight while having fun.
Wilkes-Barre, PA; Return to Glory Wilkes-Barre City's return to glory
Geoffrey Parsons' Epoch... The Land of Fair Play Better than the original.
The Bill of Rights 4 Dummmies! This is the best book to learn about your rights.
Sol Bloom's Epoch …Story of the Constitution The best book to learn the Constitution
America 4 Dummmies! All Americans should read to learn about this great country.
The Electoral College 4 Dummmies! How does it really work?
The All-Everything Machine Story about IBM's finest computer server.
ThankYou IBM! This book explains how IBM was beaten in the computer marketplace by neophytes

Amazon.com/author/brianwkelly
Brian W. Kelly has written 182 books.
Thank you for buying this one.

www.ingramcontent.com/pod-product-compliance
Lightning Source LLC
Chambersburg PA
CBHW072241290326
41934CB00008BB/1371